Local Government
and Public Service
Reform Initiative

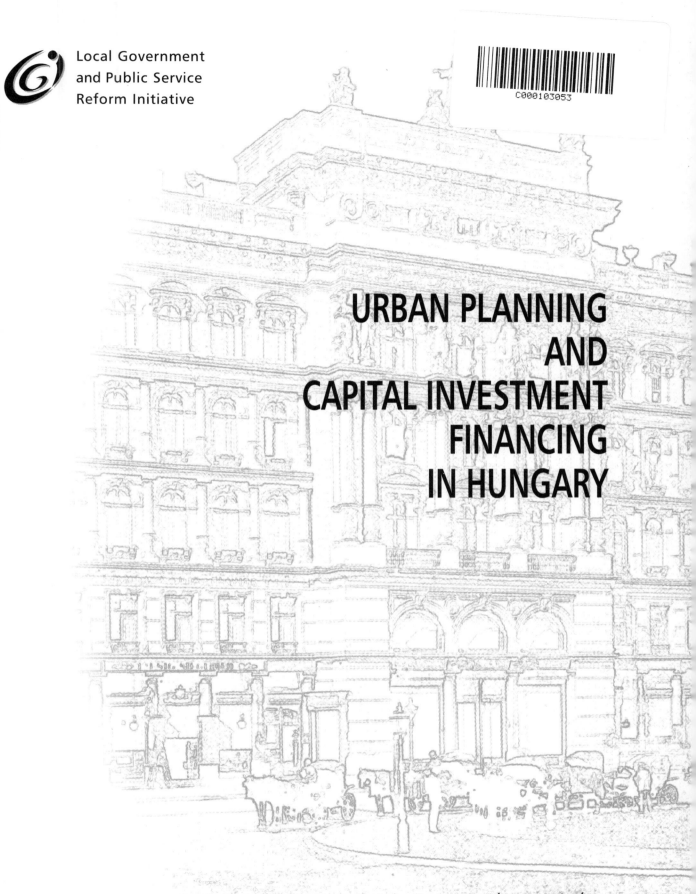

URBAN PLANNING
AND
CAPITAL INVESTMENT
FINANCING
IN HUNGARY

GÁBOR LOCSMÁNDI
GÁBOR PÉTERI
BÉLA VARGA ÖTVÖS

OPEN SOCIETY INSTITUTE
LOCAL GOVERNMENT AND PUBLIC SERVICE REFORM INITIATIVE

Address
Nádor utca 11.
H-1051 Budapest, Hungary

Mailing Address
P.O. Box 519
H-1357 Budapest, Hungary

Telephone
(36-1) 327-3104

Fax
(36-1) 327-3105

E-mail
lgprog@osi.hu

Web Site
http://www.osi.hu/lgi

ISBN: 963 00 3798 X

Second edition

Copies of the book can be ordered by e-mail or post from OSI.

Printed in Hungary, June 2001.
Design & Layout by Createch Ltd.

Contents

List of Tables and Figures

TABLES

FIGURES

Purposes of This Study

This study focuses on urban development, which is defined by four types of local government activities: (1) urban planning and regulations, (2) local government property management and (3) utilization of municipal service delivery rights and competencies, which are closely connected to (4) local government capital investment— the narrow meaning of development. Here, when discussing various aspects of these four components, the primary question is *how they are linked to one another.*

Local governments with well-integrated assets management will be able to improve their services and their financial position. In order to link these four areas, a deeper understanding of each element of urban development is required. This work began with a detailed analysis of rules, traditions and practices. Then local ways of operation were compared with available models and internationally accepted methods of management and financing. An investigation was initiated to determine the impact of sudden change on municipalities in different situations: how they reacted to such challenges and what methods have been developed. Six municipalities were examined—*Balatonboglár, Biatorbágy, Eger, Kecskemét, Tatabánya* and *Veresegyház*— of different sizes, positions and locations, and the results of the investigation are presented throughout this work. There are many lessons that can be drawn for both levels of government: at the national level concerning changes in policymaking and in the behavior of central departments, and at the local level concerning new procedures, management practices and financing schemes.

The research and development work of this study was performed under the assumption of an emerging and solid *market environment.* Local governments should identify roles and functions that are separated clearly from the private sector while simultaneously pursuing cooperation with private actors. Municipalities have to find their way under these circumstances; when private ownership is dominant in the economy, there are no major additional financial sources from privatization or from the transfer of state-owned property. Cooperation in the market system requires transparency and greater involvement of the general public in local decisions. Thus, public and private partnerships have to be based on institutions that meet the needs of both parties. Under these new circumstances, public sector operations and management should be modified as well.

Thus, local government *assets are used in a broader sense* here, including not only municipal property but also other local capacities that provide returns from local activities. Urban planning, regulations and administrative powers might have an impact on local revenue raising and thus should be regarded as assets. Similarly municipal service delivery rights can be utilized in such a way that private partnership leads to improved infrastructure and better services. Finally, local revenue policy measures are also assets. Urban development should be based on the harmonized use of these four types of assets.

Urban development as a complex activity requires *cooperation among various professions*: property and real estate managers, urban planners and regulators, local government and company finance experts. These experts do not communicate easily, and local government administrative structures often do not support such cooperation.

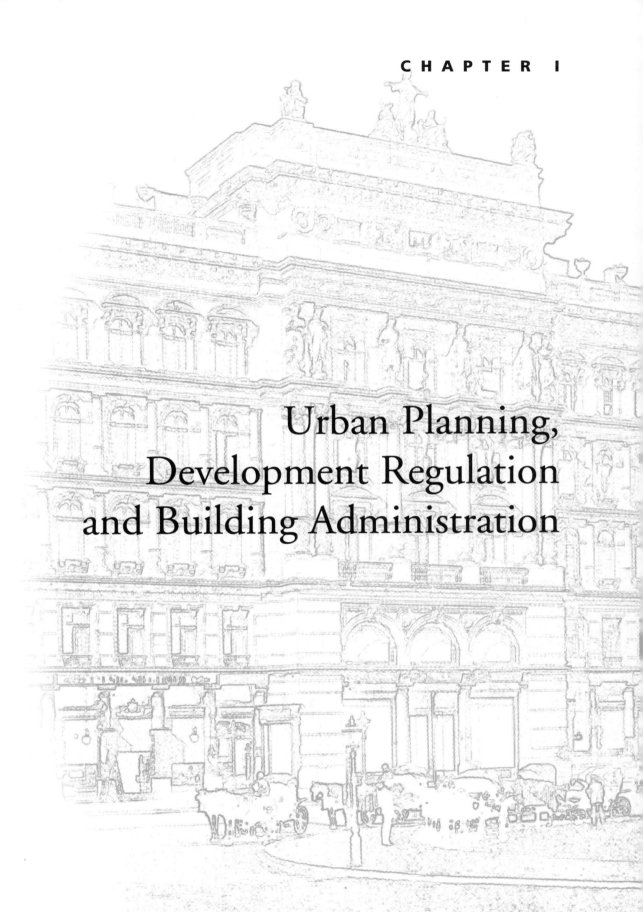

CHAPTER I

Urban Planning, Development Regulation and Building Administration

1   Urban Planning

1.1   HISTORICAL BACKGROUND

Since the end of the last century, the main emphasis of urban planning in Hungary has been the creation of "regular building plots" by well-controlled subdivision procedures (the German *Umlegung*) and a clear separation of public space (streets, squares, parks, etc.) from private land. At the turn of the century these, together with relatively simple zoning ordinances, constituted the main environmental aim of urban planning: to create an "attractive cityscape" through well-controlled building on regular plots, a kind of "City Beautiful" approach without deeper influence of the Anglo-Saxon movements of Romanticism or the "Garden City."

Zoning regulation was initiated relatively early: at the beginning of the century (the flagship of urban planning regulations) the whole city of Budapest was zoned for building in accordance with earlier German practices. Besides the simple, property owner-oriented "zoning map" and "zoning ordinances," an "official map" also existed, marking public spaces and covering the whole area of the city (both have been used in Budapest ever since, although in rather distorted forms).

Since 1881 the modified 1868 Expropriation Law enabled the community to acquire land for urban planning ("regulatory") purposes with full and immediate compensation at market prices. Preemption rights, though they existed, played only a minor role in the urban context. If cities needed large tracts of land for public purposes, in order to avoid expropriation and inflated prices, they were forced into "public speculation" through middlemen. In Budapest the legally unsound practice of avoiding expropriation procedures also evolved: if a side street was to be opened along the boundaries of two existing plots, the city could take half the width of the new street from each plot. In return the owners of the plots then were allowed to build the new "facade."[1]

In Budapest this largely contributed to the specific shaping of the overall city structure. In the downtown and inner zones, in which private property and private rental housing predominated, chances for public intervention were extremely limited (even the Opera House and the later demolished National Theater were built on existing public squares), and side streets became very narrow. Most parks, army barracks, hospitals, public buildings, industrial sites and the majority of public open spaces (parks, sport facilities, etc.) are located in a "transitional zone" between the former city border and the densely developed inner districts. The third, "outer zone" beyond the former city border also was privately owned and experienced rather uncontrolled land speculation and the construction of low-rise individual housing for the lower middle class and blue-collar workers.

1.1.1 The 1937 Urban Planning Act

In the interwar period the heavy financial burden upon most cities and a revival of the Georgist approach led to the adoption of a new urban planning act.[2] In 1937, five years before the Uthwatt Report was published in the United Kingdom, the new act authorized local governments to regain part of the betterment in an indirect way.

The 1937 act introduced a two-tiered urban planning framework: a comprehensive "general" plan under strict ministerial control and a "detailed" plan for areas where development was adopted and facilitated by the local legislative board. Based on German practices urban land (the whole administrative area) was to be classified as "building" or "nonbuilding"; in the latter, even subdivision was prohibited if the resulting plots would be smaller than eight hundred square meters. Although these new regulations considerably increased limitations on private property rights, no compensation rules and payments were introduced similar to those stipulated by the British Town and Country Planning Act of 1947.

Compensation was planned as a "short-cut" process among the affected property owners themselves in the course of the administrative procedure of plot subdivision (the German Umlegung). However, based on the Expropriation Law yet without accomplishing the expropriation procedure, the community was entitled to obtain land for public purposes free of compensation to the value of the potential gains of the property owners. From this latter point plot subdivision was classified by three categories: (1) *subdivision* of a large piece of land for building plots, (2) *correction* of plot boundaries and (3) *regrouping* of an already subdivided area.

This categorization reflects the historic occupation patterns of agrarian land. Consolidation of landed properties was not carried out universally in Hungary; at the urban fringe in many cases growth occurred in areas subdivided into long strips of agrarian land (orchards, vineyards, vegetable gardens, etc.) owned by individuals and ill-suited for building purposes. This pattern sharply differs from American conditions, where large agrarian holdings usually enable private development in large blocks, the use of private access road systems and the "private provision" of services and urban amenities.

As subdivision of a larger area for building purposes potentially could be most beneficial for the owner (developer)—i.e., the potential betterment was the highest—one-third of the land ("one-third area rule") could be taken by the city free of charge along with an additional one-fifteenth for other public purposes (public buildings, parks, etc.). The same system prevailed for regrouping, which was accomplished through the "temporary" and theoretical unification of landed properties. The affected owners were obliged to compensate each other according to original and final land values. If the taking affected an owner in an unfair way—e.g., land for a new road was taken away only from the owner on one side of the street—the obligation for compensation once more had to be assumed by the affected beneficiary—the owner on the other side of the street ("half-road area rule"). If the community failed to accomplish the public development project in three years, the obligation to compensate property owners came into force.

The plot subdivision procedure was to be carried out by the state-controlled building authorities upon request of the majority of property owners or of the city itself in close cooperation with the land registration office. Cities had to open "compensation accounts" to the credit of which payments by the "winners" were deposited and to the debit of which compensation to the "losers" was paid. Cities were authorized to pay compensation in an amount not exceeding the total sum of payments made by the beneficiaries.

The 1937 act was an interesting attempt to solve the betterment-compensation problem by integrating it into the public planning process. In contrast to similar and simultaneous efforts made in Europe, its approach was more pragmatic and practical. Based on the assumption that the affected owners shared a common interest—i.e., building permission was refused if the plot was not "regular"—the 1937 act was an attempt to keep processes within professional and bureaucratic circles and as far as possible from the courts. In conservative prewar Hungary, although a relatively modernized country, the British idea of "nationalizing development rights" would have been too sophisticated and too "leftist" an approach. The 1937 act survived the last forty years as a ministerial decree in a rather distorted form. The most surprising point is that most later alterations were made in favor of private landowners. The explanation for this follows.

1.1.2 Partial Nationalization of Landed Property after World War II

Nationalization—or rather, confiscation of private land—in Hungary was not completed under the communist era. In cities the main goal was to eradicate the ideologically unacceptable private rental housing system; consequently, the land under the inner city tenement blocks also became state property. Small owner-occupied and some rental housing units, although in many cases taken away from their former owners, usually were not nationalized. As a consequence of this and in sharp contrast to the typical western pattern, the majority of public land was concentrated in the central areas of cities, while in the outskirts—often in the most ecologically favorable sectors—housing and land remained private. A typical example is the former vineyard area of the Buda Hills in Budapest.

Consolidation of agrarian land was carried out by forcing smallholders into agricultural cooperatives, first in the 1950s and later in the 1960; thus, large estates usually surrounded the developed areas of cities. Nevertheless, this pattern was not exclusive; later members of cooperatives were allowed to have their own "household plots" (small land holdings for subsistence, market gardening and farming), and some portions of the cooperative's land—usually those less feasible for large-scale farming—were subdivided for hobby gardening and recreational purpose (a typical Hungarian mixture of the western "second home," the German "hobby garden" and the Russian *dacha*). In many cases these areas also were situated close to the city borders.

This radical transformation in ownership patterns obviously left its mark on the regulatory framework of planning. Although holding some truth, it would be an oversimplification to say that planning regulations limiting property rights lost authority on public land and gained momentum on private land. What happened was a gradual adaptation of planning to the new situation. Urban planners began to act as "salesclerks," or prioritized agents, of state-initiated developments (large-scale housing, urban and housing redevelopment, industrialization), while on private land, development control measures aimed to maintain a balance between the growing pressure for land from individual house builders and the lack of infrastructure in these areas (which was provided almost exclusively for state development). In Budapest the *Gründerzeit* repeated itself in a distorted form: then, private builders of the inner city tenements—and in bygone years, state developers—enjoyed the privilege of public provision of infrastructure, while in both periods owner-occupied house building, as a matter of fact, was deprived of it. Before demonstrating some environmental consequences of these processes the so-called "socialist" planning system will be elaborated.

1.1.3 Hungarian Urban Planning after World War II

In order to understand better both the distortions of past years and recent dilemmas in Hungarian planning orientation, this discussion will be placed in an international context based on some cross-country research. Before mentioning some procedural elements, the substantial-structural side will be summarized.

Planning mechanisms of the industrialized countries differ in at the least two distinct ways: (1) *scale* and (2) *orientation*. "Scale" refers to comprehensiveness (i.e., large-scale vs. small-scale), and "orientation" to the public and private nature of planning. The third element is the legal and *constitutional position* of planning tools and procedures (i.e., for whom plans are legally binding, who has the right to initiate changes, etc.). Based upon the first two variables, "types" of urban plans and planning procedures can be classified into four distinctive categories: (1) *comprehensive plans*, (2) *zoning plans*, (3) *detailed* (land use and/or building) *plans* and (4) *development permit procedures*. The existence or nonexistence of the fourth tool reflects the constitutional position of a nation's planning system; development permit procedures are used only in countries where landowners (developers) are authorized to apply for changes in planning regulations or at least to initiate a use of land and/or a way of building that satisfies their own interests.

In table 1 the "more comprehensive" or large-scale plans are situated on the left-hand side; "less comprehensive" or more detailed, small-scale plans are shown on the right-hand side. More public-oriented tools are found in the upper half; the less public-oriented or more private-oriented tools can be found in the lower half of the table. Comprehensive plans (a) can be best exemplified by the German "*Flächennutzungsplan*" (preparatory land use plan); the British "*structure*," "*local*" or "*unitary development*" plans for zoning (b), the extensively used American "*zoning*" and the recent system of Budapest can be listed as examples. Typical tools of detailed planning (c) are the German "*Bebaungsplan*" (legally binding land use plan) and the Dutch "*Bestimmingsplan*"; and finally the "*development permit*" procedures (d) constitute the central element of the British system, while in the United States the "*subdivision review*" and "*site development review*" procedures also fall under this latter category.

In most countries planning systems have only two "strong elements" based on historical factors, on the country's overall orientation towards private property rights and taking into account the constraints of the legal system. Finally, in order to avoid overcomplication, nations developed their planning mechanisms using two more or less interrelated basic tools. Leaving aside the supplementary (not binding or preparatory) elements, the planning systems of the United States can be placed into the lower part of the chart (b–d, or private-oriented), of Germany, into the upper one (a–c, or public-oriented), of Great Britain, on the NW–SE diagonal (a–d, or mixed orientation). Although this classification says little about the regulatory content (the degree of stress on land use, environmental, architectural, developmental, social, etc. elements) of the tools, it helps in understanding the Hungarian system that is now in transition.

Despite forty years of socialism Hungary's position in the late 1980s can best be shown on the horizontal line between the public- and private-oriented halves of the chart. As shown earlier, Hungary has followed the Central European or German model by traditionally using a comprehensive, general plan (*általános rendezési terv*—ÁRT) and a detailed plan (*részletes rendezési terv*—RRT). From both substantive and procedural aspects, these two tools were subjected to a strict hierarchical order, and both were legally binding to some extent. The large-scale ÁRT was an intricate mixture of a comprehensive plan and a zoning plan, while the small-scale RRTs were established for areas in which the fixing of land use types and zoning and building regulations required more

Table 1
Different Orientations of Urban Planning Systems

1. TYPES BY ORIENTATION AND SCALE		
Urban Planning System	Large-scale Plans	Small-scale Plans
Public-oriented	a. comprehensive plans	c. detailed land use and building plans
Private-oriented	b. zoning plans	d. development permit procedures

2. UNITED STATES OF AMERICA		
	Urban Planning System	Large-scale Plans Small-scale Plans
Public-oriented	a. comprehensive plans	c. detailed land use and building plans
Private-oriented	b. *zoning plans*	d. *development permit procedures*

3. GERMANY		
Urban Planning System	Large-scale Plans	Small-scale Plans
Public-oriented	a. *comprehensive plans*	c. *detailed land use and building plans*
Private-oriented	b. zoning plans	d. development permit procedures

4. UNITED KINGDOM		
Urban Planning System	Large-scale Plans	Small-scale Plans
Public-oriented	a. *comprehensive plans*	c. detailed land use and building plans
Private-oriented	b. zoning plans	d. *development permit procedures*

5. HUNGARY IN THE LATE 1980S AND EARLY 1990S		
Urban Planning System	Large-scale Plans	Small-scale Plans
Public-oriented	a. comprehensive plans (ÁRT)	c. detailed land use and building plans (RRT)
Private-oriented	b. zoning plans (ÁRT)	d. development permit procedures (RRT)

detailed planning. In ÁRTs those areas where "RRT-making" was obligatory were indicated, which meant that no building permit could be issued until RRT approval by the municipal council. Any alterations to plans were subject to publicly initiated local government actions; i.e., individuals and private actors were not authorized to apply for changes in the plans or to fix detailed building regulations through RRT making if RRTs were missing or were obsolete.

Although this system resembled the recent German models of Flächennutzungsplan and Bebaungsplan, there were important deviations. From a legal point of view the most important difference was that in Hungary, both ÁRTs and RRTs might *directly affect* property rights. Land use classifications permitted in both types of plans were set forth in a national zoning and building code (*Országos Építésügyi Szabályzat*—OÉSz). In this national code,

zoning classifications and the detailed building and land subdivision regulations were arranged according to a hierarchical order of allowable land use categories and subordinate building and nonbuilding zones. Localities were authorized to adopt more detailed regulations within the maximum and minimum limits of the national code. Thus, in areas where no further RRT making was prescribed by the ÁRT, the comprehensive plan worked as a zoning plan as well. This contrasted with the German model, in which the comprehensive plan, similar to the American one, is preparatory without directly affecting individual properties. This is why the boxes with bold letters, representing Hungary's previous planning system, were put in an intermediate position on the left part of the chart.

The bolded area on the right side of the chart shows the result of changes since the early 1980s that accelerated after 1990, especially with the onslaught of privatization. Under state planning RRT making in the majority of cases followed the initiatives of the state developers. As private developers began to emerge, missing or obsolete RRTs became a serious impediment to development and building. A ministerial decree authorized local governments to introduce the practice of "persuading" developers to finance official state and local government planning—i.e., to pay for the RRT making with the condition that the selection of the consultant planner remained the responsibility of the local authority. Obviously this was a step towards the British development permit or the American subdivision review, though without introducing their procedural elements (for instance, the institutionalized "bargaining" for planning gains).

1.1.4 Urban Development Patterns and Their Environmental Consequences

Although adoption of urban plans was the responsibility of municipal councils, strict central control of planning existed through direct intervention by ministerial agents and by professional juries supervised by the ministry. Even more importantly, the financing of local developments was accomplished through redistribution from central sources to counties according to regional development priorities and in a sectoral manner through the various ministries. State-initiated multistory housing and industrial development were priorities, but in the county capitals, through a second phase of "selfish" redistribution by the county councils (under political control of the party organization of the county), other sectors—e.g., traffic, office and commercial developments—also played a role. As a consequence, urban plans gradually became documents of lobbying for state grants rather than representing actual local needs. Because these grants were in limited supply and an oversimplified concept of "effectiveness" prevailed, urban development became rather centralized from a spatial point of view as well. The rate of suburban growth has not surpassed that of the core in a single Hungarian city, excluding Budapest.

This centralized development pattern had disadvantageous environmental consequences both in the inner city and in the rural-urban fringe. An abundance of state-owned property—built usually in low densities and relatively old—facilitated radical *redevelopment programs* in the downtown areas of many cities in the country. In many cases the traditional urban fabric of private and public

spaces also disappeared, giving way to a disorderly and badly maintained mess of semi-public and private territories. The scale of radical redevelopment was restricted only by its high cost due to the obligation of the local councils to rehouse tenants of the demolished state-owned rental flats. Although radical redevelopment projects tried to avoid the expropriation of private properties, in many cases it was unavoidable. As public opposition against expropriation increased, the Expropriation Law was supplemented by sections regulating compensation in kind—i.e., through the provision of housing from state sources.

In Budapest ownership patterns were reflected clearly in redevelopment activities. While in the inner city radical intervention was suspended because of high densities and rehousing costs in the late 1970s, the central parts of many of the older communities around the former (1872) city border (Újpest, Kispest, Pesterzsébet, Óbuda, etc.), also part of a program to create new "subcenters," fell victim to mass housing. Here the low-rise and low-quality rental stock and the less prestigious owner-occupied housing stock could not hold out against the overheated state redevelopment programs.

The majority of *mass housing*, however, was implemented *on green field or vacant sites*. In Budapest since the 1960s large estates of five to ten thousand units were built on public land in the semi-vacant transitional zone (between the dense inner city and the 1872 border), where due to geodesic conditions the land was unsuitable for individual, plot-by-plot development. On the rural-urban fringe, land was provided through politically influenced transactions with agricultural cooperatives and other state property owners. Land for building was in relative abundance until the late 1970s when regulations were introduced to protect farmland from development.

These regulations made it obligatory for cities to pay a redemption price to the state budget resulting in an increase in land costs. This together with the growing share of privately financed owner-occupied multilevel housing (condominiums) and the emerging feasibility considerations and decreasing state subsidies to state builders increased physical densities. The sad consequence of this was that in the new residential areas built in the 1960s, blocks of small—less than fifty square meters on average—state flats were surrounded by a relatively attractive local environment with an abundance of open spaces, while the better quality and larger residential units of the

1980s were built in estates in which the local floorspace ratio sometimes exceeded 2.0.

The overambitious redevelopment and building programs also were supported by a *construction and land subdivision ban*. Developed areas that were assigned for radical redevelopment were rezoned in the RRTs for high density building, which actually meant "regulatory taking" from small private property owners unable to participate in the state programs. No obligation for compensation was imposed on cities for this "planning blight." As this regulatory taking would last for decades, and in order to at least partly "compensate" the losses of the adversely affected private property owners, the national zoning and building code (OÉSz) precisely regulated the magnitude of maintenance and enlargement permitted in areas devoted to redevelopment. In the case of areas where state ownership was in the majority this special regulatory taking contributed, however, to neglect of building stock awaiting demolition or radical redevelopment. In Budapest this largely contributed to the deterioration of vast inner city areas.

The proportion of *single family house building*—i.e., individually initiated construction of owner-occupied houses and condominiums—*in the outskirts of cities* and villages increased continuously during the 1970s and comprised about one-third of total construction in the 1980s. The planning mechanism, which almost exclusively supported the state-initiated housing projects built in larger estates, was unable to follow these changes. In the *rural-urban fringe* growing demand for individual house building was met by a step-by-step subdivision of the land of agricultural cooperatives for building sites. No "master plans" for larger areas were established; subdivisions lacked any kind of amenities and open spaces. In most cases the public infrastructure, including street paving, was provided only later. A continuously growing share of the cost of infrastructure was imposed upon private builders, because limited and gradually decreasing financial sources were used for state-initiated housing and other developments. In the absence of a clear-cut taxation system, responsibilities of the local public authorities were unclear, and inhabitants saw this procedure as being unfair. Similar problems emerged in those areas where a gradual *transformation of land use from agrarian to urban* took place, especially in former vineyards, orchards and vegetable gardens. Here development pressure was increased by the demand for land on which the upper and upper-middle classes could build houses or condominiums. Vast *second home districts* also began to emerge in areas beyond the city borders.

In response to all these changes, the reluctance of public bodies to intervene in the "private affairs" of the more well to do became discernable. Although the 1937 building act, in the form of a ministerial statute, survived during the socialist era, it was deprived of most of its mechanisms that before the war had helped public initiatives promote environmentally more favorable development. The so-called "publicly initiated land subdivision" procedure was prohibited; initiation of land subdivision remained the exclusive right of interested property owners (this will be discussed at greater length below). The opening of new streets in order to replace old paths or widen existing ones was made more difficult, as all "takings" were subjected to expropriation (eminent domain procedure) even if this was in the interest of the majority of owners. The one-third rule and the one-half road rule of the 1937 act also were invalidated. Municipal compensation accounts were not set up; authorities had to return to the semi-legal practices of the turn of the century. The only way that expropriation could be avoided was if public officials could induce the affected owners to renounce their compensation claims for land taken away for street opening or widening. More complicate cases were left to the civil courts.

Concepts of "betterment recoup" or *Ausgleichsbetrag* were out of the question; private gains from the sharply increasing land values were lessened only by the imposition of the costs of public infrastructure upon owners. Adverse environmental effects of these processes were most serious in Budapest's "inner green belt" in the Buda Hills. Residential districts in the hills lacked any open space, and beyond the forest belt vast areas of hobby or "subsistence" gardening with dachas were developed. This latter area lacked any planning. When primary roads were built here and in other parts of the city, the necessary regrouping of the adjoining plots rarely occurred. A countrywide consequence of these processes has been massive soil erosion as well as the pollution of ground water due to a lack of sewage systems.

No deeper sociological explanation will be provided here for the hypocritical behavior of the communist state: radical intervention and unquestionable takings on one hand and a withdrawal from conflicts with the "stronger," more influential group of private property owners on the other.[3] More important is that this hypocritical behavior of the state has tended to strengthen private property rights in the view of the general public. This became obvious when, in 1990, work on a new urban planning and building act began.

1.1.5 The 1964 Act on Building

The primary legal document regulating urban development, planning and building was the Act on Building enacted in 1964 and supplemented in 1968 by a government statute. This act comprised only the major elements of planning and building law; some very important regulations were included in other documents—e.g., a 1983 ministerial statute regulating the "plan-making" process, the role of the affected authorities, organization of public hearings, the national code (OÉSz) and a special code for Budapest (BVSz). The introduction of the 1964 act determined the duties of the building administration (regional physical planning; urban planning; control of building, maintenance, renewal and demolition of physical structures; control of research; establishment of standards; preservation of historic buildings; etc.). It regulated the mandatory types of physical plans (regional and urban development programs and binding plans of controlled development—i.e., ÁRT, RRT) and the general rules on the local adoption of plans and public participation.

Only the basic regulations affecting property rights were included in the act under the *section on land subdivision* and the *section on construction and land subdivision ban*. In this respect the 1964 act partly followed the 1937 act. It stated that, with exceptions determined by the national code, no building or land subdivision was permitted beyond the officially set border of the area assigned for building. All construction had to comply with the ordinances fixed in the urban physical plans and those included in the national (Budapest) code. *Compensation* for losses in area (not value) of a plot through land subdivision measures was referred to the Civil Code by the act; no detailed or specific compensation rules were established. No compensation for any bans due to urban planning measures was ordered, neither for regulatory takings nor for bans in specific, individual cases ordered by the building authorities. A weak section recalled the spirit of the 1937 act that permitted cities to *utilize* a part of *a landed property for the purpose of public roads* without carrying out the expropriation procedure and also to avoid compensation if the affected parties renounced their claims for compensation.

In 1991 and 1992 some sections of this act were revised, abolished or changed by the newly elected multiparty Parliament and the newly established Constitutional Court, but basic changes were introduced only in the section on building and land subdivision ban. According to the new regulations *only a three-year ban was legalized*.

After this period, annual compensation amounting to five percent of land value was paid if the ban was in force on 1 January 1992 or was introduced after this date. Later, in order to relieve the burden on local governments, bans that were "introduced in the interest of the affected owner" and those made unavoidable by natural and other hazards were excluded from cases that required compensation.

These changes in the act came as a shock for planners and for the public administration. As the legal concept of "ban" was not defined, it was interpreted in extreme ways.[4] Most planners were unknowledgeable concerning legal affairs, and foreign legislation and practices were known only in small circles of academics. Lawyers made preparations for a new boom of clients, but the general public remained relatively silent. Although some property owners in the most prestigious areas in the Buda Hills began to compare recent RRTs with prewar plans, the number of court cases related to building bans remained insignificant. Finally a Constitutional Court decision made the situation clear by stating that regulatory takings did not fall under the concept of ban; only those specific cases were compensated in which the ban was ordered by the authorities.

Another Constitutional Court directive clarified the *legal status of urban plans*. ÁRT was classified in the 1991 Act on Local Governments as a preparatory land use plan binding exclusively for local governments in their decision-making processes. RRTs became the binding land use plan in the development control procedure. This meant the readoption of the "continental" approach to planning—actually, the German system.

1.1.6 New Act on Urban Planning: Dilemmas in Approaches

Although the legal position of urban plans was clarified, some elements remained matters of dispute. In the traditional, architect- and planner-dominated Hungarian system of planning, RRTs were also site development plans, including the sizes, locations and heights of the specific buildings on a plot, the formulation of which is the role of owners and private developers in many countries. Some planners thought that introducing only a single type of binding land use plan, necessarily including only the most important regulations, would result in a *lessening of architectural-environmental control* of large-scale developments. They mentioned intricate situations in overbuilt inner cities, in the recently privatized industrial areas and in green field developments as cases in which more detailed plans and control mechanisms were needed. Others argued for and worked on more sophisticated, computer-aided, intricate regulatory systems, with emphasis on environmental issues, that could overcome this problem.

This debate, closely linked to the private-public orientation dilemma, was at the heart of the legislative work on *a new Act on the Formation and Protection of the Built Environment* in the Ministry of Regional Development and Environment. The debate boiled down to the dilemma of whether to adopt Anglo-Saxon or continental orientation. Supporters of the former approach proposed the introduction of a kind of development permit (or a "site development—subdivision—review") procedure as the third control mechanism added to the system of ÁRTs and RRTs. They argued that such a tool existed in the past: larger state development projects beyond the authority of the local government fell under the obligation of a "*land use permit procedure*" that was not abolished after the transition.

It also was stressed that the emergence of private development, together with the lack of financial means for public infrastructural development, resulted in a great number of unofficial "bargains" between cities and private developers in order to obtain some planning gains for the community. Although some earlier versions of the text of the new act included this type of control mechanism, the final version enacted in 1997 shows a return to the simple two-tiered system of a preparatory comprehensive ("structure") plan and a binding ("regulatory") plan.

1.2 URBAN PLANNING AND URBAN PHYSICAL PLANS

The 1997 Act on the Formation and Protection of the Built Environment abolished the traditional two-tiered system of general and detail plans and, following the German model, introduced three planning tools—namely, the *structure plan*, the *regulatory plan* and the *local planning ordinance*. Although these names may be familiar to foreign readers, it must be stressed that they cover concepts slightly different from those of their European and American counterparts. Thus, a short overview of the evolving new Hungarian system of spatial-physical planning is needed.

Responsibilities and mechanisms of spatial-physical planning in Hungary can be arranged best along two main variables: spatial dimension and planning function. Considering the spatial dimension, plans are *regional* ("territorial" in Hungarian) and *local*; from the point of view of their operation they can refer either to *development planning* or *development control* (see table 2).

This simple model reflects the old institutional and professional division in Hungary between urban and regional and also between economic and physical planning; this division was accentuated further under the state economy in the last forty years. Urban economics have never been an integral part of spatial planning in Hungary, while architect and planner involvement in regional physical planning has become rather significant since the 1970s. Even now state administrative control of spatial planning in Hungary is divided between two ministries: regional development planning and control and municipal development control fall under the Ministry of Agriculture and Rural Development (until 1988, the Ministry of Environment and Regional Development); local development planning, with its strong financial bearings, falls under the Ministry of the Interior.

The main concern addressed in this study involves the lower part of table 2, particularly concerning local development control mechanisms. As indicated by the table,

Table 2
Spatial Planning in Hungary

Spatial Dimension	Development Planning	Development Control
Regional	Focused on regional economics	Principal infrastructure and land use elements in regional plans are to be considered in local plans
Local	Long-range concepts of physical development and capital improvement programming	Focused on regulatory mechanisms, zoning, land subdivision, building administration

structure plans in Hungary have nothing to do with the comprehensive plans used in, for example, the United Kingdom and the Netherlands, where these plans cover urban regions or counties and are controlled by regional administrations. As will be shown later in more detail, the Hungarian structure plan is a "nonmandatory," comprehensive, local land use plan that may cover only the administrative area of the municipality, while regulatory plans are "compulsory" zoning and building plans.

It also must be added that in the past ten years regional physical planning largely has been overshadowed in Hungary by the reestablished autonomy and powers of the municipal governments and by the diminished authority of the county governments. Former regional physical plans (the National Settlement Network Concept of 1971 and the plans of the nineteen counties, among others) were abolished. Until 1997 when a new Act on Regional Development and Planning was adopted and county and regional development councils were established, no regional concepts and plans diminished the authority of local governments in formulating their own concepts and in adopting local plans.

1.2.1 Goals of Planning

According to the new act, the main tasks of local physical planning are threefold: (1) creation of a well-ordered and well-coordinated physical environment, (2) promotion of the operational capabilities of cities and villages through the effective utilization of their resources and endowments while minimizing environmental nuisances and (3) protection of those characteristic and valuable structural and built elements of cities and villages—including cityscapes and landscapes—that warrant preservation.

Although these main functions of urban planning codified by law are essentially physical (order, appearance, well-run operations, preservation of amenities and resources), Hungarian lawmakers adopted from the German Building and Planning Act a long list of additional requirements that have to be met by plans and that put physical planning in a much broader context. In the preparation of plans and the performance of development control activities, attention is paid in particular to the following:

- general requirements for healthy living and working conditions and for the safety of the population;
- healthy demographic development and housing requirements of the population;

- physiological, mental and psychological needs of the population, particularly those of families, the young, the elderly and the handicapped, including educational needs, sports, leisure and recreational facilities;
- requirements of social organizations and churches;
- economic requirements that ensure acceptable income and consumer supply for the population, including protection and creation of employment, of the interests of agriculture and forestry, of transport, of the postal and telecommunications services, of public utilities (particularly power supply and water, waste disposal and sewerage) and of natural resources;
- defense and civil defense requirements;
- utilization of suitable natural resources for medical purposes.

It also is emphasized in the new act that in the process of planning, public and private interests are to be balanced ("according to public interests with regard to lawful private interests").

Half a year after the adoption of the new Urban Planning Act this goal-setting—an almost literal translation of the corresponding sections of the German urban planning law—seems to be nothing more than a manifest declaration of values in planning. Involvement of courts in planning matters, excluding expropriation (eminent domain procedure), have been rather rare in the past forty years; no plans or zoning ordinances were weighed against such values. Since 1990 if a local plan or regulation was challenged, the Constitutional Court determined the issue based on much broader legal considerations included in the Constitution.[5] Nevertheless, as private property development becomes prevalent and the involvement of courts in planning matters grows, broader social and economic effects of planning decisions gradually will come to the fore, and concepts like "exclusionary zoning" and the like will be discussed more frequently.

1.3 COMPREHENSIVE STRUCTURE PLAN

As demonstrated earlier the traditional Hungarian system included both a general and a detailed plan; this model was abolished by the new act. The main difference between the new and old systems is that in the past, both general and detailed plans included compulsory (zoning) elements. A substantial part of the general plan was actually a zoning plan for areas where the zoning ordinance could be applied easily to private landed properties; for other parts of the city the general plan included only a prescription that a detailed plan be accomplished and adopted later. For these areas the detailed plan served as a combined zoning and building plan.

1.3.1 Legal Status of the Comprehensive Plan

According to the new act the comprehensive local plan is called the *structure plan* (*településszerkezeti terv*) and is actually a *preparatory land use plan* with few zoning elements. The act includes another comprehensive planning tool: the *urban development concept*, which is to be adopted before the creation of the structure plan and is a more "verbal" and socioeconomic-oriented document. The new Act on the Formation and Protection of the Built Environment is not an American-type "enabling act"; it makes the preparation of the concept and the structure plan *mandatory for all municipalities in Hungary* together with binding planning elements.

The leading idea behind this system is to introduce two groups of interrelated planning documents that, however, clearly are separated from each other from a legal point of view: (1) the development concept and the structure plan are to be adopted by the board of representatives (legislative board) of the municipality through a *legislative decision* and are binding only for the board itself; (2) those documents that define actual *development rights* for the property owners (the regulatory plan and the zoning and building ordinance) are adopted by the same board by a *municipal statute*, i.e., through a *legislative act*.

1.3.2 Content of the Structure Plan

The structure plan represents the developmental potential and directions of the municipality—basically, the type of land uses and the spatial arrangement of the main infrastructural elements in accordance with intended urban development. It is stressed in the act that overwhelming national and regional interests, development rights of the surrounding and other municipalities affected by the plan and environmental requirements are to be taken into consideration in the plan. At minimum the structure plan shall represent:

- the official boundary between the "inner" and "external" area of the municipality;
- building and nonbuilding land (both can be designed in the official inner and external areas);

- main spaces and boundaries of public interest (main distributors, parks);
- protected areas and those that are designed to be protected, special defensive zones;
- areas for which uses are planned to be amended;
- existing and planned public utility mains.

Spaces and their uses that are affected by harmful or other external factors, especially by mining, natural and artificial holes below the surface, pollution, flooding, soil erosion or shifting and land for which no central sewerage provisions have been made, are to be represented.

Although the legal status of the nonbinding structure plan and of the binding regulatory plan(s) (and of the ordinance) basically differs, *all types of planning instruments must use the same land use categories*. However, two important distinctions should be kept in mind:

- in the comprehensive structure plan *only the maximum floorspace ratio* permitted for various land uses *is to be defined*;
- although the nonbinding structure plan does not serve as the legal basis for building administration, *even in the lack of a binding plan or ordinance, construction permits are to be issued* (if the proposed structure complies with the standards of the building code and with all other regulations) based on the structure plan and considering a simple rule: the proposed usage of land and the manner of building shall "*fit into the surrounding, existing environment.*"

Despite different legal statuses of planning instruments, lawmakers wanted to achieve continuity in the hierarchy of plans by actually *merging the elements of comprehensive planning and zoning*. The 1997 act on urban planning also indirectly induces municipalities to elaborate their comprehensive and binding plans in one uniform parallel process. This reflects the old Central European tradition and is characteristic of the German planning law and practice that has been used as a model by Hungarian lawmakers. There is a trend in Hungary to extend zoning to the whole administrative area of cities and villages in order to effectively "regulate" property development everywhere. This is actually a definite move towards the American *dominance of zoning*.

1.4 BINDING REGULATORY PLAN

Since 1997 the binding land use plan in Hungary is called a *regulatory plan*. As will be seen in more detail later, the concept of a regulatory plan *may cover both a*—relatively simple—*zoning plan and a more detailed plan* similar to the German Bebaungsplan or the American "planned unit development." Although municipalities are induced to "regulate" development everywhere, it is not mandatory for them to elaborate regulatory plans for their whole territory. However, it is prescribed by law that regulatory plans for the following be established:

- areas assigned to *new development or redevelopment* (e.g., urban renewal, rehabilitation);
- areas that *require special attention* due to their natural endowments, valuable physical urban structure, architectural heritage or specific use (e.g., recreational areas or health resorts of high priority);
- in cases when it is deemed *necessary for the "order" of building.*

The regulatory plan can be prepared *for the whole administrative area* of the municipality or for *a definite part* of it, but this part *cannot be smaller than a block* (a group of lots bordered in most cases by streets). This extreme diversity in the allowed spatial extension of the planning process and documents needs some explanation.

There was a definite fear among some lawmakers in the Ministry of Environment and Regional Development about the potential oversimplification of planning by using only a zoning-type instrument in binding land use plans as proposed by others. There were multiple reasons for this concern. It could be argued that some forms of urban projects in the public interest (e.g., urban renewal) require a more sophisticated and detailed planning process. On the other hand, in Hungary (and also in Germany until the reintegration of the eastern provinces) *discretionary procedures of reviewing* and controlling larger and more *complicated urban projects* (e.g., the British development permit or the American site development review) *never have been introduced.* It also has to be stressed that in Hungary zoning and subdivision ordinances traditionally are not separated as in the United States; thus, by adopting a binding urban plan the legislative board may decide on a great number of intricate "planning details" as well. The outcome can be annoying for a foreign observer: the extreme variety of urban plans in spatial extension will remain unchanged in Hungary.

In Hungary urban plans traditionally contain *two types of documents*: those that are *to be enacted by the legislative board* and those that *support and explain* binding elements of the plan. According to the 1997 act, planning documents that are for legislative adoption include *a map* that contains the regulatory content of the plan (on a scale of 1:1,000) and the *ordinance.*[6]

1.4.1 Standards Determined at the National Level

Since 1990 there has been a trend towards "deregulation." In urban planning this trend could not come to the fore due to the delay in the adoption of the new act (five years since its first version was drafted in 1993) by Parliament; as a consequence, until the end of 1997 the mandatory content of plans was determined by a 1983 ministerial decree. Two concepts dominated the long process of lawmaking: *to restrict private property (development) rights* by means of planning *to the slightest necessary degree* and *to assign the majority of "regulatory power" to local governments.*

As late as 1997 the lawmakers' idea was not to render any type of land use or zoning category as mandatory for the local regulatory plans—i.e., all "zoning power" was delegated to the municipalities. In the end, based on Hungarian tradition and on the German model, *a list of land use categories was introduced* by the National Planning and Building Ordinance (OTÉK), a government decree in force since 1 January 1998. As already mentioned, the total administrative (both inner and external) area of municipalities is to be divided into *building and nonbuilding land.* Mandatory land use categories are arranged in OTÉK according to these two types based on a simple rule: for building land, the lot coverage index is to be at least as high as ten percent; for nonbuilding land, this figure cannot be higher than five percent—a regulation introduced in order *to facilitate compactness* of urban development.

Land use categories included in the structure plan are to be specified by zoning districts in binding regulatory plans. Land for building is to be specified by "*zoning districts for building,*" while land use categories for nonbuilding land are to be specified by "*zoning districts.*" Municipalities are authorized to prepare their own zoning districts and zoning ordinances *within the restrictions* provided by the national ordinance.

1. *Land use categories in areas assigned for building*

See table 3.

2. *Nonbuilding land use categories and zones:*
- transport, public utilities, telecommunication networks;

Table 3

Zoning and Land Use Categories as Prescribed by the State Planning and Building Ordinance [1997]

Defined in the Structure Plan			Defined in Regulatory Plans (Ordinance)		
General Use	Specific Use	Maximum Floorspace Ratio	Maximum Lot Coverage [%]	Maximum Height of Structures [m]	Minimal Landscape of the Lot [%]
Residential	high density urban	3.0	80	12.5<	10
	medium density urban	1.5	60	<12.5	20
	low density (garden city)	0.6	30	<7.5	50
	rural	0.5	30		40
Mixed	city center	2.4	80		10
	core areas	3.5	max. 25 % above the highest lot coverage of land in residential use		half of the undeveloped part of the lot
Commercial	retail and services	2.0	60		20
	manufacturing with substantial adverse impacts	1.5	30		40
	other manufacturing	1.5	50		25
Recreational	resort hotels, camps	1.0	30	6.0<	40
	weekend houses	0.2	20	<6.0	60
Special		2.0	40		40

- open spaces, parks;
- forests
  — for protective purposes,
  — for commercial purposes,
  — for health care, social and tourism purposes,
  — for education and research;
- agriculture;
- other uses.

In *open spaces and parks* building coverage may not be greater than two percent; in *forest areas* for commercial purposes or for education and research—0.5 percent; in forest areas for health, social and tourism purposes—five percent, but only if the size of the building lot exceeds ten hectares. For agricultural land national standards are set in a more complicated way: *in areas with vineyards,*

orchards and vegetable gardens (a classification of agrarian land used also in the land registry) *one dwelling* is permitted if the lot exceeds three thousand square meters; in areas of other agrarian use—six thousand square meters. *Non-residential farm buildings* also are allowed on lots that are larger than seven hundred twenty square meters.

Before World War II almost any structures beyond the "inner area" of municipalities (a border set by a strictly regulated administrative procedure) were prohibited. Since the 1960s small lots have been subdivided for subsistence gardening and recreation, modeled after Russian-type dachas. In the 1980s a revival of traditional farmsteads took place in the Great Plains of eastern Hungary. After 1990 landowners whose agrarian property was confiscated in the 1950s were recompensed in most cases by land located close to developed areas. All these factors led to a relaxation in national regulations for "external" areas. The final step in this direction was indicated by the new act and OTÉK, which permitted the assignment of zones for building outside developed areas, rendering the administrative border between external and inner areas of municipalities irrelevant in planning matters.

1.4.2 Mandatory Elements of Regulatory Plans

According to OTÉK *municipalities must specify some elements* in their regulatory plans and ordinances, while a limited number of other elements may be introduced as well. In zoning districts for building *it is compulsory* that the following be specified:

- minimum size of building lots;
- form of building (detached, semidetached, etc.);
- maximum lot coverage index;
- permitted minimum and maximum height of structures;
- improvement standards of public utilities as a precondition to construction;
- minimum size of open space per lot;
- environmental impacts requiring permits, emission/immission (e.g., noise);
- rules of construction below the surface.

In zoning districts—nonbuilding land—only two elements *are permitted* for local regulation:

- form of building;
- permitted maximum height of structures.

In both zoning districts for building and zoning districts *it is permitted* that the following be regulated:

- determination of the "exclusivity" of use;
- minimum width and length of building lots if required to preserve the characteristics of the cityscape and city structure, as well as other aesthetic and architectural control measures;
- regulatory measures concerning linear structures and their facilities (e.g., roads).

1.4.3 Permitted and Not Permitted Uses

The above concepts can be misleading to a foreign reader. In Hungary *no administrative procedure of use permission exists*. The concept "permitted use" refers to those that, according to lawmakers, *are not in conflict with the general*

use of a land use category or a zoning district (e.g., a building of the municipal administration in a high density residential zone); thus, they are allowed by the regulatory plan in a specific area. These permitted uses, together with those *that are not permitted* in specific zoning areas, also are determined by the nationwide OTÉK. *Authorization for the determination of exclusivity of only one use* in both types of zones, however, provides an overall exemption from the general rule.

On this point the 1997 act and OTÉK are not clear enough, and this later may lead to some confusion. In urban plans enacted before 1990 it was typical that some areas were designated for only one specific public use —e.g., a zoo or party or trade union headquarters. Exclusivity of use may refer to this kind of designation as well. Another problem is that a "partial exclusivity" might occur—i.e., only a group of permitted uses are excluded locally from a zoning district. The concept of permitted use—together with that of uses permitted only in exceptional cases—was borrowed from the German Land Utilization Ordinance (*Baunutzungsverordnung*). The German law provides—by zones and in extremely detailed form—broad authorization for including or excluding both permitted and exceptionally permitted uses in plans. The Hungarian law, instead of providing detailed regulation, only refers to the dubious concept of exclusivity.

Another important innovation in Hungarian law was borrowed from U.S. planning "ideology." It is stipulated in OTÉK that both land use categories (in structure plans) and zoning districts (in regulatory plans) are to be assigned according to a "*homogeneity principle*": "Based on their existing or planned function, development and character, zoning districts are to be established in a way that within a specific zoning district all landed properties shall be vested with the same development rights and obligations." This new rule was introduced primarily *to satisfy the equity principle* and to prevent the regulation of building lot by lot, a fervent preoccupation of architect-planners in recent years.

It is impossible here to give a whole list of the *permitted, exceptionally permitted and not permitted uses* in all zoning districts; only some examples will be given. According to OTÉK *petrol stations* are permitted exceptionally in all residential districts excluding high-density residential districts, where they may be built only as part of multistory parking garages. *Hotels* are permitted in all residential districts excluding garden city districts. *Shops* and nondisruptive commercial operations, including pubs and restaurants, serving the everyday needs of the population are permitted in all residential districts. In *garden city districts* residential buildings with *not more than four dwellings* generally are permitted, while buildings with not more than six dwellings are permitted only in exceptional cases.

In *mixed use areas* the distinction between zoning districts of the "*city center*" and "*core areas*" is made according to the *relative position of residential use to other permitted central functions*: in city centers only nonresidential structures that do not have substantial adverse effects on residential use are permitted. In core areas this protective measure for housing does not exist. However, in order to preserve residential use in core areas municipalities are authorized by OTÉK to introduce measures prescribing that on specific floors or in specific parts of nonresidential structures, only dwellings may be built; this authorization also has been borrowed almost literally from the German law.

"*Special use*" districts are to be established for uses that *require protection* against substantial adverse effects and that may be *disruptive to their surroundings*. Among these special uses mentioned by OTÉK are shopping malls; sites for trade fairs; exhibition, convention and congress centers; areas for educational, health care, research and development and renewable energy (wind and solar) institutions; areas for national defense establishments; zoos; mines and quarries; and sites for waste disposal and waste processing.

1.4.4 Map of the Regulatory Plan

The regulatory plan must contain a map that indicates all *binding elements* of the plan as well as those *that are "recommended" or are "for consideration" by the building authority* when performing its administrative procedures (building and subdivision permission are the most important). The following are considered binding elements on the map:

- right-of-way widths (called "regulatory lines" in Hungarian);
- borders of both land use areas and zoning districts;
- symbols indicating the land use and zoning classification of the area, including
  - the relevant land use category and zoning district,
  - building form (detached, semidetached, etc.),
  - site coverage index (percent),

  - maximum and minimum height of structures (in meters),
  - minimum size of building site;
- lines indicating where one or more building fronts are fixed by the regulatory plan ("building line" in Hungarian);
- borders in each lot (area) within which structures are permitted to be built;
- trees and vegetation that are to be preserved;
- trees and vegetation that are to be planted.

Individual (building) lots may not be indicated on the map as binding elements. A regulatory plan roughly can determine only the density, height and form of building in an area together with permitted uses and the mapping of those areas where some important environmental standards prevail.

In the past a sharp distinction was made between two types of building sites: those that were called "*individual*" and were assigned for only one single structure, and those that were for allocating more buildings—in the majority of cases, large-scale, modernist housing developments. The latter were called "block lots," and their areas had to be distinguished and represented on the map. Some standards in the national ordinance were set differently for the two types of lots. By abolishing the distinction between the two, lawmakers attempted to extort high flexibility in local plans; this also means that the American "cluster development" automatically is permitted in Hungary. As will be shown later, however, this leads to some complications, because in Hungary subdivision control is a purely administrative procedure performed by building authorities without discretionary powers.

In a regulatory plan those elements of the structure plan must be represented that have bearing upon matters of natural and cultural heritage preservation and environmental control: e.g., areas of architectural heritage, archeological sites, historic gardens, architectural monuments, biotic reserves, national parks, nature conservation areas (national and local), noise control zones, mines, holes below the surface. On the forthcoming pages details of the maps of three regulatory plans are presented indicating that binding local plans in Hungary may serve quite different purposes. Consequently, their mapped content also may be substantially different. Compared to the U.S. practice, some may be similar to a simplified "preliminary subdivision plan," others to the maps of a planned unit development or of a site development plan.

1.5 MUNICIPAL ZONING AND BUILDING ORDINANCE

This local ordinance is enacted by the municipal board of representatives through a legislative act: *a local government statute*. In the view of lawmakers the ordinance is the *primary planning document* of a municipality, while the regulatory plan(s) is a *complementary document* in which spatial implications of the ordinance are mapped. Municipalities are encouraged by ministerial officials to establish the *ordinance for their whole administrative area* (both external and inner zones) by adapting the national ordinance (OTÉK) and through regulations of local relevance as authorized by OTÉK. According to the 1997 act regulatory content of the local ordinance corresponds to that of the regulatory plan(s) but also must include those standards that, not permitted to be mapped, can be expressed only "verbally"—e.g., minimum size of building sites. In theory *local standards cannot be "less rigorous" than national standards.*

Although municipalities are encouraged to establish local ordinances for their whole administrative areas, it is permitted by the 1997 act, in the same manner as that concerning regulatory plans, to prepare and enact a *local planning and building ordinance for a single block* as well. If municipalities establish a citywide ordinance, it is doubtful that they later can establish a more detailed ordinance (and regulatory plan) for a smaller part of the city. It is to be expected that local planners will follow a method "invented" in many municipalities in recent years: as part of their "old" general plans, they enacted citywide ordinances by zoning districts, and after more detailed plans were adopted for specific areas, planners integrated their regulations into ordinances of general plans.

This method, however, provides a basic divergence from the previous parallelism of general and detailed plans that in many cases left areas of cities without any regulation until a detailed plan, prescribed by the general plan, was adopted and enacted. Although not included in the 1997 act and OTÉK, a reasonable solution would be that the *citywide ordinance* include all regulations and standards that determine basic development rights—those that *primarily influence development value* of a piece of land —while the ensuing regulations of a regulatory plan refines standards according to the specific endowments of the site. In all likelihood, this solution will be used in Budapest.

1.6 THE SPECIAL CASE OF BUDAPEST

According to the 1991 Act on Local Governments, twenty-three district governments function in the Hungarian capital, plus a twenty-fourth—the municipal government of Budapest, which is the local government of the entire city. Responsibilities are divided between the municipal government and the district governments and are determined by the 1991 Act on the Capital; for example, responsibilities for the building and maintenance of main roads that carry public transportation fall under the municipal government, while other roads fall under the district governments. The division of responsibilities is complicated by the fact that the district governments are not subordinate to the government of the entire city. This situation is reflected in the planning system of Budapest as well.

According to section 14 of the 1997 act on planning and building, special provisions are applicable for Budapest. In short, "zoning power" is divided in Budapest between the city and its districts. This is a major divergence from the previous situation, when the city possessed all zoning authority and districts could establish detailed plans only if their regulations were in conformity with citywide zoning or if the municipal government accepted changes in zoning districts proposed by district plans. The 1997 act introduced a special binding plan under the authority of the municipal government of Budapest—the "*framework regulatory plan*"—and an ordinance for the entire city, while the districts are authorized to establish their own "*district regulatory plans*" and ordinances. Contrary to the equal policy-making authority of the city and its districts, *urban plans of the districts are subordinate to the citywide plan.*

In the framework regulatory plan of Budapest binding components are determined that affect the whole city or more than a single district and that affect the responsibilities of the municipal government established by law. These components are:
- borders between the inner and external areas;
- the marking of building and nonbuilding land for the whole city and the division of the city into zoning districts (though the scope of standards that can be set by the city is limited);
- marking all public areas—e.g., thoroughfares and main roads—that are necessary for the reasonable operation and functioning of the entire city;

- special purpose areas owned by the municipal government (e.g., parks);
- areas and structures for conservation or special protection;
- infrastructural network mains;
- marking of areas that fall under "special legal institutions" as noted in the 1997 act (to be discussed later).

These elements of the framework regulatory plan are applicable in the regulatory plans of the districts, and any amendments of them by the districts must be accompanied by amendment of the citywide plan: i.e., the municipal government must accept the change.

The new, nonbinding structure plan of Budapest was adopted in 1996, and it took two and a half years for an agreement to be reached between the city and its districts concerning the actual content of the citywide binding plan and its ordinance. So-called "*framework zoning districts*" were established that determine loose standards, providing "space" for the districts to ascertain specific local requirements. In the end the framework regulatory plan and the *framework zoning ordinance* of Budapest were adopted by the general assembly in August 1998, though the documents have not yet been made public. As a result of this legislative process, it can be expected that three types of binding plans and zoning documents will have parallel functions:

- the citywide framework regulatory plan and ordinance;
- the district zoning ordinances (in compliance with the framework ordinance);
- district regulatory plans (if more "sophisticated" regulations are needed and in compliance with the district zoning ordinance).

It is not quite clear how this three-tiered system will be established and will function. Consultant planners who worked on the framework plan and ordinance think that in individual cases the framework zoning ordinance will serve as the basis for building administration. If a district establishes a district regulatory plan, its ordinance, with its specific standards, will be integrated into the citywide ordinance, and step-by-step the whole city will be "covered" by the relevant plans and regulations. This is complicated by the fact that after 1990 many districts of Budapest actively established old-type detailed plans for their whole area, which will not be revised for a while (more on this

topic is discussed later). Other districts decided to establish their own zoning ordinances immediately, based on the framework ordinance.

In the case of Budapest national lawmakers did not follow the German model. In Berlin, for instance, only the preparatory, nonbinding land use plan (Flächennutzungs-plan) falls under the domain of the municipal government; binding land use plans are prepared by the districts. Compliance of the latter to the citywide plan is controlled by a procedure in the competence of the city alderman responsible for urban planning and by the simple rule that this control is to be performed only if the area in question is larger than three hectares.

The rigidity and high complication of the Budapest system can be explained, first of all, by the unique administrative system of the Hungarian capital and the resulting—in many cases, political—tensions between the city and its districts. Another important aspect is that in Hungary there now is greater confidence in plans—i.e., in planning documents "carried out"—made effective through well-controlled administrative procedures than in discretionary procedures performed by any body other than the legislative board. In previous years even applications for minor zoning amendments regarding only one single lot submitted by the districts had to be adopted by the seventy-two elected members of Budapest's general assembly. The same attitude is prevalent concerning those new planning mechanisms that were introduced as the most important innovations in Hungarian urban planning law: special legal instruments.

2 Special Legal Instruments of Urban Development

Legal tools were introduced by the 1997 act in order *to facilitate the implementation of urban plans.* If a municipality is willing to utilize a legal institution, in most cases it is included in the regulatory plans and in the local zoning and building ordinance. Such tools include the following:

- *legal requirements of building*—permissibility;
- *development freezes*—building and other types of bans;
- *land subdivision*—subdivision permit;
- *municipal preemption rights;*
- *rules of compensation;*
- *designation of land for local roads*—dedication of land;
- *expropriation*—eminent domain procedure;
- *contribution to the expenses of public infrastructure*—fees in lieu of dedication;
- *enforcement of obligations*—binding plans and regulations.[7]

These instruments are not actually new innovations; most were included in the 1937 act on building. As most major urban developments in the past forty years were carried out or effectively guided by state or municipal agencies, these types of legal tools were used only in favor of the state developer, as was the case with expropriation. Regarding "special legal institutions," the 1997 act is actually a simple "enabling act" that outlines only the basic rules with few references to the relevant legislative or administrative procedures. The results of the case studies revealed that few of the municipalities analyzed have considered introducing any of these tools; thus, a short description of them would be satisfactory here.

2.1 PERMISSIBILITY OF BUILDING

As a general rule, *on land assigned for building* any such activities *must occur on building sites.* A building permit is issued only if the lot in question conforms to the standards established in the local ordinance and is accessible (by vehicle) by a public or private road. Concerning *non-building land* broad discretionary power is delegated to authorities issuing building permits: within the confines of the national standards (e.g., land coverage index in OTÉK) they determine if the construction violates public

interests; has adverse effect on land values, soil or water management; blocks accessibility of neighboring areas; and has specific use, which cannot be designated for building land.

2.2 DEVELOPMENT FREEZES, BUILDING AND LAND SUBDIVISION BANS

These types of instruments rarely are utilized in Anglo-Saxon practice but have been applicable in Central Europe and Germany for a long time. The concept of *development freeze* refers to the safeguarding of the planning process against developments presumably in conflict with the proposed plan. Municipalities may opt to add a development freeze *by issuing a local government decree* for the area covered by a proposed regulatory plan and local ordinance. The freeze is terminated as soon as the reasons for it cease to exist or three years from the date of its adoption. In areas under the scope of development freeze *no new structures may be established* and no redevelopment, expansion, demolition of or value-adding alterations in existing structures is permitted excluding cases of "threat to life." For three years no compensation is paid to the affected parties.

Contrary to development freezes *building and land subdivision bans are administrative actions* of the building authority *introduced by an administrative decision* issued individually to those *actually affected* by the ban. Affected parties may lodge an appeal against the decision; in cases of development freezes, this option does not exist. This type of ban predominantly is used *to prevent natural or environmental hazards.* For example, a building ban was introduced in the 1980s around Balaton when the lake's water quality was endangered by the lack of adequate sewage networks in surrounding cities. Under building or land subdivision bans, more is permitted by the 1997 act than under development freezes: building activities in compliance with the future use of the area, demolition of structures, maintenance activities, conservation and renewal of protected buildings, archeological research, activities of environmental management and extension of a dwelling by not more than twenty-five square meters.

Until 1990 no compensation was paid for losses to owners of property under building or subdivision bans. When *in 1990 a requirement for compensation was introduced* by an amendment to the 1964 Act on Building, which remained in force until 1997, cities terminated most of those regulations in their plans that served as bans as well as those that were considered as *regulatory takings* ("planning blight" in the United Kingdom). Few of them are expected to alter this behavior in the future.

2.3 LAND SUBDIVISION

This term too can be misleading for a foreign reader. In the United States the purpose of subdivision regulations and of the corresponding processes—i.e., subdivision review—is to exercise effective control over development. In Hungary the term subdivision review refers to a less complex activity. It is a purely administrative process that ensures that land is split into parcels, the characteristics of which (area, width, shape, etc.) are in compliance with the regulatory plan and ordinance. The task is performed in most cases by a single official of the *building authority* or, in larger cities, by a group of trained surveyors who *upon application issue subdivision permits.*

As mentioned earlier, the 1937 Urban Planning Act was actually a national enabling act on subdivision. It regulated compulsory land dedication requirements for roads imposed on subdividers, their responsibilities to provide land for public facilities (schools, parks, etc.) and rules on how land was to be reallocated among affected owners when an existing plot was planned for redivision for building sites. Contrary to the United States the need for redivision has been frequent in Hungary. On the fringe of the developed areas of cities, instead of large tracts of land, usually small lots for agrarian use are found, the original layout of which rarely can be used for allocating urban functions.

After World War II subdivision control of large state housing developments was carried out by the public developer itself—in most cases, a municipal development company—in collaboration with the responsible municipal offices and agencies (the leading office was the municipal department of urban development). Official urban plans were amended often as required by evolving building programs; administrative permit processes, albeit effectuated in the majority of cases, lost importance. Parallel to these processes public involvement in the subdivision of private land also decreased. Since after the transition most municipal development companies were privatized

and private development accelerated, subdivision has been left without an effective control mechanism (efforts to reestablish this are discussed later).

Currently the process of land subdivision permission is *regulated by a 1971 government decree*, a new decree is expected this year. The 1997 act includes a *list of relevant forms of subdivision*: (1) redivision of a group of existing lots, (2) subdivision of a lot (tract) into smaller lots, (3) unification of lots and (4) "regulation" of lot boundaries (minor amendments between adjoining lots). As decisions on all special legal institutions are represented in the regulatory plan, areas where substantial replotting or subdivision is needed are shown on the map of the plan indicating that an application for *a subdivision permit is required in advance of a building permit*. Without going into detail the 1997 act authorizes municipalities to delegate the cost of improvement that is needed to accomplish the subdivision upon the applicant.

3 Building Administration

In this section *administrative permit, inspection and enforcement activities* will be discussed as performed by various authorities. First, activities of the building authorities will be elaborated in more detail. Only a brief account can be given of the tasks of other authorities involved in urban development, and an example of the permit process concerning public utilities will describe how various authorities and public agencies cooperate in Hungary.

3.1 THE BUILDING AUTHORITY

From 1990 to 1997 building authorities operated even in small villages. In order to ensure adequate professional staffing, the 1997 act ordained their *concentration in cities* leaving the rights of villages to establish their own authorities untouched, provided that they cooperate and prove that the *staff has adequate qualifications.* A municipality not operating a locally based office is notified of and may appeal against all decisions of the relevant building authority.

A great number of *other agencies* are involved as well. Administration of a broad set of construction activities, such as networks of roads, railroads, airports, telecommunications, electric power, district heating, pipelines and storage tanks of petrol and natural gas, mines, nuclear plants and waterworks, is performed by other agencies, some of which *also act as special purpose authorities* in matters that fall under the responsibility of the building authorities. Construction and maintenance of *networks of water supply, drainage and sewage* fall under building authorities provided that the relevant public utility company declares that the necessary level of service can be supplied.

Special purpose authorities are involved in administration *upon request of the building authority.* They may *give or deny consent* in matters concerning their limited responsibilities based on law and in matters not regulated by binding local urban plans and ordinances. Decisions of special purpose authorities are incorporated into the response issued by the building authority. The *building authority also may act as a special purpose authority* in matters outside its scope; in such cases it only may examine whether or not the intended development project complies with OTÉK

and with the provisions included in the local regulatory plan and ordinance (based on the principle of "noninterference" with the responsibilities of other agencies).

3.1.1 Limited Discretionary Powers of the Building Authority

As mentioned earlier, *OTÉK defines detailed provisions for planning/zoning and building* (a detailed description of the latter is outside the scope of this paper). The main task of the building authority is *to enforce these provisions* and also those local rules included in the regulatory plan and ordinance. It is, however, obliged to examine thoroughly issues such as ensuring the "protection of the cityscape and landscape, of architectural and urban character," the requirements of "favorable orientation" of buildings and rooms, the "regular maintenance of specific buildings" and that the "nuisances caused by the use of the building will not exceed permitted levels." Requirements of this kind, although detailed in OTÉK, cannot be circumscribed precisely; thus, building authorities are given some discretionary power in these matters. The 1997 act makes explicit reference to such authority by enabling municipalities to ordain applications for *preliminary building permits* mandatory in specific cases (more on this is discussed later).

3.1.2 Construction Subject to Building Permit

A 1997 government statute gives a clear description of those building activities and structures that require a building permit. As a general rule a building permit is necessary for *the construction of new buildings and the extension or removal (demolition) of existing structures.* A building permit is also required if a structure under the obligations of a building permit is *to be renovated, reconstructed, altered or modernized,* but only if such activity affects its *structural elements or outward appearance,* or if the *number of distinct units*—the number of dwellings— or their use is to *change* (to give an example, the unification and conversion of two flats into an office requires such permission). A building permit is required for all shop windows, for establishing advertising lights, for displays exceeding one square meter and for modification of the ground area of a lot exceeding one meter in height. A detailed list of *structures and installations not requiring building permits* is also included in the statute; some examples include solar panels, small wind generators, customary backyard recreational facilities and pools less than ten square meters in size. Detailed rules exist for the disassembly of such structures as well.

3.1.3 Permits Issued by the Building Authority

In Hungary building authorities may issue the following types of permits:
- preliminary building permit;
- building permit;
- demolition permit;
- occupation permit;
- "permit to stand";
- use amendment permit.

One important type of permit is not mentioned here: the *land subdivision permit* is issued by the building authority according to a 1971 government statute and is expected to be amended soon. Some of its basic problems will be discussed later.

Preliminary building permit

The task of a preliminary permit is "to *clarify in advance the requirements* of ... architectural character, archeology, urban heritage, cityscape, environmental protection and natural conservation, eliminating dangers to life ..." As building authorities are obliged to collect documents of consent issued by most of the special purpose authorities and agencies (excluding those of most public utility companies, which are to be obtained by the architect) a preliminary permit *provides developers with valuable information* on the specific requirements for their projects. Through a regulatory plan and ordinance municipalities also may *render an application for a preliminary permit compulsory in predetermined cases.*

The cities and villages studied tend to use the latter to control more complicated developments similar to the U.S. planned unit development or cluster developments through preliminary permit procedures. The need for a preliminary permit may occur in simpler cases as well.

Since a regulatory plan cannot include "final" subdivision, sometimes it is impossible to regulate precisely the layout of structures on "yet unknown" building sites; once more a preliminary permit made compulsory in these cases may be of assistance. The main reason for the increasing use of preliminary permits was discussed earlier: the 1997 act abolished the two-tiered system of binding urban plans—ÁRT and RRT—and no procedures similar to the U.S. subdivision review or the U.K. planning permit have been established.

Many municipalities, including some districts of Budapest, are concerned with relying too heavily on decisions of building authority staff with the parallel relinquishing of discretionary powers of commissions and of the legislative board. They think that some intermediate procedures are needed; where planning/zoning control actually "ends" and where administrative control of building and construction "begins" is not defined clearly yet by law in Hungary.

The preliminary permit *is binding for both the building authority and the involved special purpose authorities* up to one year from the date of issuance but is invalidated if no application for a final building permit is submitted during this time period. *No construction may be initiated* based on a preliminary permit. The preliminary permit also can be issued *with conditions attached.*

Building permit

The contents of an application for a building permit are similar to those for a preliminary permit: plans, declarations of consent of public utility companies or agencies, a declaration by the architect that the plan conforms to the relevant regulations and standards and that he or she is licensed, a statement by an architectural and planning jury if needed by law and an *environmental permit* if the project is subject to an *environmental impact study (EIS).* One additional document is included with an application for a building permit: a *use permit* issued by the land utilization office *if agrarian land is targeted for construction.*

Another important deviation from the rules of the preliminary permit process is that if the building authority discovers that *the relevant building site has been established*—plotted—*according to the regulatory plan and ordinance* and related provisions, land subdivision precedes the building permit. The *builder* also must prove that he or she *is entitled to build*—i.e., is the owner of the building site.

Similar to a preliminary permit, the building permit also *may be issued with conditions.* Conditions set by the building authority or by special purpose authorities may be stricter than the standards included in ordinances and administrative decisions of general validity, and deviations also may be approved. Conditions other than those of the preliminary permit can be set only if the general rules of OTÉK or the regulations of local plans and ordinances have been amended in the meantime. A building permit can be issued *for temporary structures* as well; such decisions include the conditions under which the *obligation of demolition, removal or rebuilding* of the structure can be enforced *without compensation.*

A positive decision on an application for a building permit includes a notice that, if *a liable, licensed architect* is not assigned to the site, the building authority is entitled *to issue an order to stop construction* and that the builder is responsible for informing the building authority of the *date of the geodesic demarcation of the structure.* The decision of the building authority is disclosed to the builder, the architect, the special authorities involved and the *immediate neighbors of the building site.* The latter and the builder can *lodge appeals* against the decision.

The building permit *is valid for two years*—i.e., construction starts within two years from the date of permit issuance and must be *accomplished within another five years.* It is possible to apply for an *extension on the validity* of the permit annually; if the builder does not do so, construction may continue only if a new building permit is issued. It is also possible to apply for a *variance permit* if the builder wants to make small amendments in the course of implementation. General rules of the *demolition permit process* are the same as those concerning building permits.

Occupation permit

The occupation permit is issued to verify that a permitted structure has been built according to the approved plan and can be used properly and safely. If the *safe use of the structure is not guaranteed* or the construction activities have caused *dangerous adverse affects to an adjoining property,* the building authority may *withdraw the occupation permit.* Declarations of consent of the involved special purpose authorities and of the public utility companies or agencies are attached to the application for an occupation permit. The building authority makes its decision after carrying out an on-site inspection. The permit can be given *with conditions* as well. Should minor

deviations from the approved plan or less important defects caused by imperfect construction be found, the building authority may *issue an enforcement order* together with a *warning of prospective penalty* if the required corrections are not made. A *provisional occupation permit* can be issued for a completed portion of a structure. The same affected parties, agencies, authorities and persons are notified according to the same procedures as those for a building permit. After such procedures are concluded the builder is obliged to present an *"as-built" plan* to the land registry office.

Permit to stand

The 1997 act on planning and building regulates this type of permit in full detail. As in former decades *construction without a building permit or without compliance with the approved plan—i.e., illegal building*—has been relatively frequent, and a complicated procedure to "legalize" completed or semi-completed structures subsequently has evolved. General provisions that enable building authorities to issue a permit to stand are the same as those discussed earlier when referring to the powers of building authorities. A permit may be issued particularly if "by rebuilding, an 'illegal' structure, or part of this structure, can be made 'legal,' or if the defects caused by the illegal construction are minor, no public interests are hurt and the defects can be averted within a specified time set by the authority." The process also can be performed ex officio at the expense of the builder if he or she does not apply for a permit to stand.

This permit can be issued in a *final* manner or it may be *valid until withdrawal or for a predefined period.* A document for a permit to stand must include what rebuilding or mitigation measures are obligatory for the owner of the property together with a decision on *levying a fine.* If there is no ground for issuing a permit to stand or the builder does not perform his or her obligations the building authority issues a *demolition order.* The building authority may act *one year after detection of the illegal building activity* and within ten years of the date of completion of construction or from the date of issuance of the occupation permit.

Use amendment permit

The rules of this administrative procedure conform to those of a building permit. If the building authority detects an illegal and permanent conversion of a structure it may *compel the user to terminate use* or to apply for a use amendment permit.

3.1.4 Fines on Illegal Building

After 1990 fines *on illegal construction* were abolished by Parliament and an *overall obligation for demolition* of illegal structures was introduced (the amount of the imposed fines was so insignificant that builders tended to incorporate expected fines into their financial calculations). *The 1997 act reestablished fines* on illegal building and determined their minimum at *twenty percent of the value of the structure* or the part of the structure completed. The maximum fine may amount to as much as one hundred percent of the total value of the structure.[8]

The fine can be remitted only if the required remedies have been performed by the final day of payment. Municipalities *cannot offer discounts* from the fine, but installment payment over the course of one year is possible. Receipts from fines on illegal building are paid into the account of the *National Environmental Fund.* Municipalities and building authorities have the same thirty percent share in the proceedings of the fund (if a second level building authority—a county administrative office—also has been involved in a procedure, it collects fifteen percent at the expense of the share of the first level authority).

3.1.5 Enforcement Orders

As discussed earlier local government statutes on regulatory plans and ordinances may include provisions on obligations of property owners in the sphere of planning control (development of a site, restoration of structures that spoil the skyline, landscaping). According to a 1997 government statute *building authorities may issue enforcement orders* for individual properties if these obligations fail to be met. Besides these enforcement orders they also are authorized to make *decisions on individual cases* predominantly concerning *building sites, structures, parts or groups of structures,* even if no such provisions are set in the binding plans and ordinances.

The building authority *may order a total or partial rebuilding* of structures if demolition is not possible, termination of use, correction of defects and maintenance and renewal of structures if it is found that recent conditions *have seriously adverse effects* on the stability of the original and adjoining structures or jeopardize life, health, public or material security. Building authorities *independently may decide* on matters such as the termination of an unpermitted use, halting construction that is not in compliance with the approved plan, the replacement of building materials or installations that do not meet relevant standards, renovation surpassing normal levels of maintenance *needed for the improvement of the cityscape* or included in binding plans and ordinances and the fencing of a site.

The enforcement order must include a *description of obligations and their consequences in full detail,* the deadline and timing for their fulfillment, a notice that lack of compliance with the obligations to develop the site *may lead to expropriation* or the owner may apply for the purchase of the property if he or she is unable to comply, and correct information on the amount of subsidies available to accomplish the required renewal or landscaping if the cost surpasses normal levels. The decision of the building authority *is recorded in the land registry* if the deadline for fulfillment of the obligation is determined to be more than one year. In the case of default the required construction may be executed by order of the relevant authority on behalf of the obligated. In the latter case expenses and relevant subsidies are covered by the National Environmental Fund. A *registration of mortgage* on the affected property is also possible if the obligations are performed by the order of the building authority.

The introduction of these rigorous provisions was necessary because no other effective fiscal mechanisms to direct urban development into desired areas was functioning in Hungary. Before World War II a property tax levied on structures existed in Budapest. Compactness of spatial development of the city was promoted by a system of exemptions from this tax: in zones close to the city center relief from property tax was given for longer periods—between ten and twenty-five years (which contributed to the overcrowding of the inner city). Promotion of development of vacant sites also can be achieved by a value-based property tax, especially if vacant sites are taxed at a higher rate. Although the introduction of such a tax is planned in the coming years, its useful effects have not been considered seriously yet.

3.1.6 Land Subdivision Permit

Until recently the building authority in cooperation with the land registry office was responsible for this administrative procedure. As discussed earlier, according to the

1937 Urban Planning Act, land subdivision constituted the central element in the implementation of urban plans: mandatory dedications, decisions on the obligations of the "winners" to counterfinance the losses of those adversely affected by the subdivision, a municipal budget that allowed intervention if necessary, the intervention of courts as a last resort in the most disputed cases—all these were conceived to perform a public service that could facilitate equity and that would relieve municipalities of unnecessary financial burdens.

According to a *1971 ministerial statute on land subdivision*, the amendment of which is expected soon, the process was deprived of most of the elements of the 1937 act that facilitated active involvement of the municipalities. The land subdivision permit has been *degraded to a purely administrative procedure, the effectuation of which depends almost exclusively on the willingness of the affected parties— owners—to cooperate* and to come to an agreement. Since the basic precondition for the issuance of any building permit is that *"regular building sites" actually have been established*, this system may act against development, mainly in areas where redivision of lots is necessary (as discussed earlier, a need for redivision is more common in Hungary than, for instance, in the United States for areas that support, for example, gardening and vineyards). A short description of the recent process of land subdivision follows.

The process is initiated upon application. If more lots or owners are affected the process begins only *if the majority (fifty-one percent) of the owners apply*. If structures are affected by subdivision, their demolition or other modifications are required and public utility lines must be rearranged according to the new pattern of building lots. As with building permits the building authority also may *issue preliminary permits* that are valid for one year. A *certification clause of the land registry office* is attached to the application for a final permit in order to prove that the relevant lot sizes, registry numbers, names of owners, etc. are correct. The building authority issues or denies the permit after considering if the proposed subdivision complies with general regulations (OTÉK) and if the provisions are included in the local binding plans and ordinances. The permit is valid for one year with the possibility for extension based on annual application.

The building authority *does not notify the land registry office* about its decisions; it is the applicant's task to apply for registration. *The building authority also does not have the power to enforce* the effectuation of its decisions;

whether or not the permitted subdivision will be implemented depends on the *affected parties* who *must enter contractual relations* before contacting the land registry office for registration. Municipalities and other *public agencies may apply ex officio* for subdivision permits *related exclusively to their public projects*—e.g., a new public thoroughfare—in most cases as *part of another administrative procedure*, such as an expropriation or land use permit.

Land subdivision recently seems to be the weakest element of planning and building administration in Hungary. Despite the fact that through this process property rights are the most closely effected, until 1998 even the smallest villages with building authorities were authorized to issue subdivision permits; trained staffs are lacking, and the whole problem has moved beyond the interest of local and consultant planners.

Both public and private parties have suffered from the negative outcomes of this situation. If opening a new thoroughfare was planned through a suburban part of a city, the municipality's competency was restricted to its own affairs—i.e., to acquire the land for the road, without any power to influence or enforce necessary land subdivision in the adjoining areas. In areas zoned for single family residential buildings a great number of landowners were deprived of building permits if one neighbor refused to sign or withdrew from the prepared contract at the last moment, and the needed street could not be opened.

Time will tell if the new provisions in the 1997 act—the minor distributor and local streets included in the regulatory plan shall be accomplished by municipalities until the occupation of the structures they serve; municipalities can register land for local roads without the consent of the affected parties—together with the awaited new statute on subdivision will improve the situation substantially.

3.2 PUBLIC ADMINISTRATION OF LISTED BUILDINGS AND CONSERVATION AREAS

The building administration of listed buildings (architectural monuments, heritage buildings) and conservation areas is performed in Hungary by agencies other than the local (regional) authorities. The *1997 Act on Monument Conservation* refers these tasks to a central administrative agency, the *National Office of Monument Conservation*

(OMvH) and to its own building authority, the *Directorate of the Inspectorate of Monuments*. Parallel to a substantial reduction in the number of listed buildings, parks and other protected elements that shall remain state property (273 altogether), the new act on monuments introduced a definite concept of *areawide control and management* of historic, architectural and environmental heritage. As a consequence, municipalities were given important tasks in introducing special provisions for *areas of conservation and protection* in their plans and ordinances.

In addition to *individual monuments* (buildings, other structures, their groups or their parts; ruins of architectural, landscape-architectural, historic, scientific, urban, artistic, archeological and technical importance), *their interrelated parts and their sites*, areawide management refers to the following:

1. *conservation areas* ("areas of monuments" in Hungarian)—areas where individual monuments are concentrated, where some urban elements, the "urban fabric," the cityscape and the landscape are worthy of protection, even if not all elements in the area are listed individually and such monuments are underground;

2. *broader conservation areas* ("environment of monuments" in Hungarian)—the surroundings of conservation areas, the development of which is subordinated to the requirements of the "core" conservation area;

3. *protected areas*—(1) and (2) together;

4. *historic gardens*—gardens or parks of historic value connected to individual monuments or to the historic urban structure of a city.

OMvH and its inspectorate are *central government agencies* under the Ministry of Protection of National Heritage that promoted recentralization followed by inefficient management during privatization of architectural and historic heritage sites. The inspectorate acts both as a first level building authority and as a special purpose authority; the president of OMvH acts with the power of a second level authority. Decisions are made in Budapest, and the inspectorate employs officials who prepare decisions based upon fieldwork in the municipalities.

3.2.1 Urban Plans and Conservation

Anybody, including primarily local governments, may initiate a request that structures and areas be placed under protection, but the final decision is made by the inspectorate. If an area has been classified as a protected area the relevant municipality *is obliged to prepare a regulatory plan and ordinance* for the area including necessary protective measures. According to the 1997 Act on Monument Conservation in these plans special attention is paid regarding the preservation or reestablishment of historic morphological character, harmonious coexistence of the protected area with adjoining areas, maintenance of the historic building, effective and undisturbed appearance of monuments, traditional landscaping and microarchitecture, traffic control that responds to the requirements of the historic environment and harmonization of new construction with the character of the protected area. These are to be effectuated in the course of the development process as well.

These plans are subject to the "expert opinion" of the inspectorate, the acceptance of which—as with all other urban plans and ordinances—rests with the elected board of the municipality; the plan can be contested only if it is in conflict with national regulations and standards. *Discretionary powers of local governments*, however, *are substantially curtailed* as the inspectorate was granted broad powers in the administration of heritage buildings and protected areas by the 1997 act.

3.2.2 The Inspectorate as a Building Authority

Concerning *individual monuments* the inspectorate acts as the first level building authority by *issuing building, occupation, land use and land subdivision permits*. These administrative powers of the inspectorate are broader than those of a local (regional) building authority, because authorization also may refer to *elements that otherwise do not fall under the requirements of a building permit* but that have some "relevance to the purpose of protective measures" and also to the planting of trees, analysis of the structural elements of buildings, archeological research, etc.

If required, a permit for the renewal or restoration of a heritage building may include specific *provisions that do not conform to national standards* or to regulations in OTÉK, but the relevant—in most cases, the building—authority is approached for consent (in such cases, the building authority acts as a special purpose authority). The inspectorate doesn't issue a preliminary permit, but it is bound to issue, on application, a *statement about the specific requirements* set as preconditions for the issuance of a permit.

3.2.3 The Inspectorate as a Special Purpose Authority

The building authority and any other relevant authorities *approach the inspectorate for consent* in the application process for a building or demolition permit *in protected areas* even if this process refers to structures or parts of structures *not classified as individual monuments*. Consent also is required in these areas for many other activities and processes, such as land utilization, land subdivision, changes in the use of public areas (roads, squares, etc.), planting and cutting trees, geological surveys, expropriations, abandonment of cemeteries and urban design elements (pavement, street lighting, display of advertisements, etc.). *In districts outside protected areas* the inspectorate is authorized to exercise control on the display of large advertisements if they block or spoil the view of a protected building or of a historic part of the city.

Such strong mandates were a reaction against the "aesthetic pollution" of the previous regime visible in the most valuable parts of cities. Some historic cities (e.g., Eger), however, have experienced a radical loss in their power to shape their urban and architectural environments on their own. They are concerned about the central areas of their cities for which a substantial part of building administration is carried out "elsewhere," sometimes based on the reports of visiting inspectors who spend only one day per week in the city.

General property rights, not directly related to development, also may be *restricted* through the actions of heritage protection agencies. Consent of the minister is needed for any transfer of the property rights of monuments in municipal ownership. Without consent of the inspectorate no monuments can be *converted into condominiums* and no *easements* may be purchased or registered on the property. If the "interests of heritage protection cannot otherwise be met" or upon request by the owner, *the property may be subject to expropriation* (eminent domain procedure). Expropriation may be requested only if it is proven that expenses override the owner's financial capabilities and subsidies, actual use is substantially and permanently restricted and no open market transfer of the property was possible in the preceding year.

3.2.4 Other Important Authorizations

Responsibilities of owners (users) to upkeep and maintain heritage buildings refer to the *entire facility,* including details, interior design and also those elements that are indispensable for actual use. *No demolition permit* can be issued for heritage buildings except for the removal of specific elements that spoil the appearance of the monument. Subsidies are available from the National Environmental Fund, but their provision is obligatory only if residential buildings are concerned.

A rigorous rule that may hinder development for a longer period is that *ruins have been extended heritage protection,* especially in areas where their existence is suspected. All actors involved in the building process are obliged to notify the inspectorate or the notary of the municipality about any findings of structures or parts of structures; after an immediate review of the site these agencies *may issue a "stop order"* for up to thirty days. Although this suspension of construction is compensated, the inspectorate may put the site under final or provisional protection. A declaration of *provisional protection* is valid for no longer than one year (with the possibility for renewal for an additional year); the owner of the property is compensated for losses in this instance as well. In order to implement its decisions, the inspectorate may issue enforcement orders and levy fines.

3.2.5 Buildings and Areas under Local Protection

According to the 1997 Act on the Formation and Protection of the Built Environment municipalities are obliged to determine "local architectural heritage" structures and areas and specific regulations concerning the manner of their protection in a local statute. As most municipalities recently began to elaborate these documents, no further comments on the issue are possible here. It is to be expected that these statutes will reflect great variety depending upon specific local attitudes.

3.3 AESTHETIC AND ARCHITECTURAL CONTROLS

Aesthetic control is one of the weakest elements in Hungarian administration of planning and building. Part of the problem goes back to the distortions of past decades: weakly controlled self construction, licenses given to "architects" with only high school or college degrees for designing single family houses, suppression of education of aesthetics in schools, poor staffing in building authorities, etc. The problem has been aggravated in recent years by the "aesthetic pluralism" of the newest architectural trends, the emergence of new urban structures like shopping malls, "secondhand" design commissioned by cheaply hired local architects for foreign firms and the collapse of a well-organized system of architectural competitions.

Additionally, the formal responsibilities of chief architects (in most municipalities the best-trained experts in this field) are in many places, especially in larger cities, restricted to the management of urban plans and ordinances, while the issuance of building permits is accomplished separately by less trained staff. The 1997 Act on the Formation and Protection of Built Environment introduced *some corrective measures*, two of which are of importance in the near future: new national regulations on architectural competitions and more stringent rules on the *issuance of architectural design licenses*. Only the new regulations on competitions and juries will be discussed in detail here.

Since in the past forty years almost all construction of national or local importance was financed publicly, it was relatively easy to establish and run a nationwide system of *planning, urban design and architectural competitions* controlled by the ministry and the Architects' Association. After the political changes private developers and most municipalities viewed this system as an illegal intrusion into their affairs. Consulting boards that advised the building authorities on design issues previous to the issuance of building permits were dissolved in most municipalities based upon a Constitutional Court decision.

For *major public purchases,* including commissions for building, a mandatory *tendering procedure* was introduced by the 1996 Act on Public Purchases. Provisions of this act focus on the procedural side of competitions without reference to architectural or urban design. Municipalities have started to *invite tenders for both design and implementation* that in many cases lead to "cheap-and-bad" results. The 1997 Act on the Formation and Protection of Built Environment complemented the provisions of the act on public purchases with the rule that the best architectural solutions for major public projects be selected through an architectural-urban design competition. The act also authorizes municipalities *to order by local statute the requirements for architectural* (also urban planning and design, garden design) *competitions* in specific cases and areas.

The Ministry of Agriculture and Country Development manages a *central jury* in Budapest that controls major

urban plans of cities of county status through limited advisory power. The same type of *jury* is *organized by each regional chief architect* (representing the ministry) concerning the plans of municipalities. According to a new ministerial decree *municipal chief architects also will be empowered* to organize juries; more detailed regulation on this is expected soon.

Most large cities also have *architectural juries* with extremely diverse powers. In Budapest a jury under the planning commission of the city government discusses all types of planning and design proposals. Its relative strength is ensured by the majority of the chief architects (planners) of the districts inducing developers and designers of the most problematic projects to present their proposals to the municipal jury that hires leading architects—and whose criticism can be rather damning.

There also is the opportunity to influence the quality of planning and design at *meetings of the planning committee* of the city of Budapest when *district proposals for zoning amendments* are discussed. As mentioned earlier, it is not yet clear if the recent adoption of the framework regulatory plan and ordinance of the entire city will change this situation substantially. Zoning power of the districts has been broadened, and presumably fewer applications for zoning amendments will be presented, consequently resulting in the weakening of power of the commission and the legislative board.

3.4 ADMINISTRATION OF PUBLIC UTILITIES AND LAND IMPROVEMENT

In the past forty years most major developments—i.e., large, multilevel residential estates—were carried out on large tracts of state-owned land by state development agencies. After the council adopted the detailed urban plan, a *development program* also was established by the local development agency and adopted by the local council. If in the course of the elaboration of these development programs a need for minor—or, in some cases, basic—changes compared to the adopted urban plan was identified (e.g., more residential units were to be built) a revision of the urban plan followed and the same council "officially" amended the plan. The positive outcome of this process was that the control of design, implementation and installation of land improvements could be well effectuated.

3.4.1 The Problem of Easements

After the political changes, as municipalities began to sell tracts of public land to private developers, a serious negative effect emerged. Former state developers tended to handle "publicly owned" sites as "public areas" (streets, squares, etc.); thus, sometimes public utility mains did not follow streets and crossed sites sold for development. Since public utility companies were privatized this problem is aggravated, as the companies' responsibilities for the maintenance and upkeep of utilities extend only as far as the border of the site. A sophisticated system of easements similar to those in the United States has not been established in Hungary; utility companies insist on easements being registered on privately owned sites, while the owners, in fear that this will decrease land value, usually resist. The most serious problems occur in industrial and commercial zones, where the rearrangement of utility lines cannot correspond to the division of land into smaller properties.

3.4.2 Land Use Permit for Public Utilities

The building authorities *issue most land use permits*. The regulatory plan of the area must include a proposal for the lines and networks of utilities (water supply, storm water management, sewage, gas, electric power and telecommunications), but without any specifications. On application the relevant agencies and companies state an expert opinion if they are able to provide the necessary capacities for the planned development. Concerning *water supply, storm water management and sewage* the process of permit is as follows:

1. *documents* submitted, including
   - construction plan with all specifications,
   - official map,
   - a certificate of proprietorship issued by the land registry;
2. *consent* given by
   - public utility companies or agencies,
   - inspectorate of the environment,
   - regional office of the national health and medical officer;
3. *special purpose agency license* acquired from the directorate of water management.

Based on the documents under (1) and consent of authorities under (2), *the directorate of water management issues a license based on the national water law,* and finally *the building authority reviews the technical matters* and issues the land use permit. It is the responsibility of the applicant to obtain the consent of all public utility companies, proving that the location of the planned utility line does not conflict with their interests. These control measures were introduced in 1995 and have been in effect since 1997. Similar procedures apply for permits for the construction of natural gas pipes and, with some important variances, for electric power networks.

4   Linkages between Urban Planning and Building Administration

In recent years most municipalities in Hungary have been rather well informed about expected changes in planning and building law. The regional chief architects, as agents of the ministry, and some top consultant planners have acted as excellent conveyors of information. In response most municipalities have followed a dual strategy: (1) formal—rather then conceptual—*adaptation to expected changes* in law and (2) local *introduction of new, innovative measures* in order to adapt their systems of planning and building administration to the requirements of the evolving market economy.

4.1   DEVELOPMENT STRATEGIES, ÁRTS, RRTS AND LOCAL ORDINANCES

According to the 1997 Act on Formation and Protection of the Built Environment, previously adopted urban plans—general and detailed (ÁRTs and RRTs)—*remain in force* until they are revised or amended officially. Those municipalities, however, that have not adopted an ÁRT (or a "unitary" urban plan, in which contents of general and detailed plans are combined—usually small villages) are obliged to adopt a new structure plan in five years. In all other municipalities a new structure plan in compliance with the new act must be established in ten years at the latest.

Provisions included in *municipal planning statutes that are in conflict with the new act must be amended* in one year. This, in principle, doesn't affect preestablished zoning ordinances, because nationwide mandatory zoning measures are regulated by OTÉK. Many municipalities, however, have commenced enforcement of some new measures in OTÉK that are "more stringent" than their previous versions, e.g., provisions concerning on-site parking in central urban areas. This *parallelism of old and new rules* may lead to some confusion.

In most large cities new general plans have been adopted in the last few years, or at least the previously established ÁRTs have been revised substantially. A frequently used method has been the *completion of the "missing" RRTs and their integration into the preestablished general plan.* In a few cases these efforts led to one single planning document and to a *citywide zoning ordinance* (e.g., in Kecskemét).

In other cities that lacked this integrative approach the *two-tiered system of plans and ordinances* remained unaltered: ordinances of the old and new RRTs were added as "appendices" to the less-detailed citywide ordinances.

Most cities have embarked on *drafting new development concepts and strategies* representing either comprehensive development policy documents or the conceptual basis of new general—structure—plans. Few of these experiments have been successful. The most effective approaches were those that *focused on a clear-cut selection of development priorities* without breaking them down to sectoral details (Eger, Biatorbágy). These strategies were able to well *identify strengths and weaknesses* of the local communities and in all probability have better chances of surviving election cycles.

In some cities (Kecskemét) public officials of the mayor's office developed strategy. Although based on correct data and factual knowledge of the basic problems of a city *an avoidance of taking sides* is characteristic of these documents together with the fact that some *important sectoral links remain undisclosed.* If consultant planners have been contracted their attitude in most cases has been "cross-sectoral," *suitably balancing economic, social and spatial elements*, and rather *innovative* as far as methods of financing, taxation, institutional settings, public participation, etc. are concerned (Budapest). It also has been proven, however, that without adequate knowledge of local circumstances (Kecskemét) consultants tend to suggest *solutions that have been tested elsewhere,* but have no local or national relevance, at least not in the short run. As the six case studies revealed, cooperation between local officials and consultants is the most successful.

Both the selection of *suitable time spans* and the *relationship of development strategies to physical plans* and ordinances and also to *short-range urban development programs* represent a basic challenge to strategy building. Most new local strategies fail in supporting long-range development visions and concepts by real *"growth management" programs,* elements of which can be introduced in the short run or at least gradually. Recently, most cities have long-range development strategies and short-range (five-year) capital improvement programs and urban physical plans without any effective measures capable of channeling urban development into the desired directions. This fact is demonstrated in the following section.

4.2 LACK OF EFFECTIVE GROWTH CONTROL IN THE URBAN FRINGE

In many Hungarian municipalities there is great pressure for green field development. As discussed earlier, the owners of reprivatized land around the perimeter of cities also support this. Despite "soft-spoken" statements in development strategies in the ÁRTs of most of these cities that favor the *compactness of spatial development,* a large proportion of agrarian land has been assigned for development. In some cities the local legislators have rejected even the vague timing of development in the urban fringe.

The example of Szombathely, the county capital of Vas (which is not among the cities surveyed in the case studies), can say a lot about this problem. The city's general plan was criticized sharply by ministerial officials when it was presented to its jury because along a new tangential road (designed to relieve the inner city from through-traffic) the whole strip of agrarian land was zoned for commercial use. Attention was called to the problems (financing and public infrastructure, among others) to be expected from the simultaneous development of large areas, some of which are removed from each other.

The mayor's reply was that *it would have been unfair to deprive any of the affected owners of the opportunity for development* of their lands. He also added that they are planning to commence development where owners give a "definite signal" of multilateral cooperation and where they are willing to pay for the infrastructure. Consultant planners of the city's ÁRT failed to recommend specific provisions that might identify such "signals" and the "willingness" of owners (a similar situation has been observed in Kecskemét).

As shown by these examples a specific political element has been introduced in Hungary: *it is impossible to manage urban growth effectively with only purely physical regulatory plans.* This acknowledgement, however, is to be transformed gradually into clear-cut programs and methods. The 1997 act provides some authorization to municipalities to add "economic regulations" to the physical ones in their urban plans—e.g., preemption rights and mandatory contributions to the expenses of public infrastructure. Few cities, however, have utilized such authority; most hesitate to embark on the politically sensitive ventures of curtailing

property rights in a differentiated manner. Such anxieties could be diminished at least partly by (1) *a better understanding of the best strategies, methods and procedures used internationally* and (2) *more detailed authorization* by law.

Better understanding is needed concerning:

- the real effects of value-based local property tax on land use matters (a new state regulation on this type of local tax will be introduced soon);
- the differing legal and economic implications of tax-based and cost-based tools (for instance, the basic difference between *dedications, impact fees* and *special assessment districts*);
- betterment through the municipality serving as a real actor, as exemplified by *comprehensive development areas (ZACs)* in France and *Entwicklungsgebiete* and *Ernäuerungsgebiete* in Germany, not only—as formerly believed—when an area is newly zoned for development;
- the specific roles and liabilities of special municipal, private or public-private partnership (PPP) development companies (those in Holland, or the German *Entwicklungsträgers*);
- the use of the most innovative growth management methods (*transferable property rights,* timely limited amount of development rights distributed according to specific standards, such as those in the United States and France);
- how a well-established *adequate public facilities test* actually works (as in the United States; this is planned for introduction in Budapest).

The 1997 Act on the Formation and Protection of Built Environment was intended to serve exclusively as the *legal framework of "planning control" and of building administration;* thus, it does not include any regulations regarding the process of those major developments that are initiated by the municipalities or are in their vital interests. As mentioned earlier, the 1997 act was modeled on the German Baugesetzbuch (building law), but none of the parts of the German law were adopted that refer to the *"implementation" of regulatory plans*—i.e., detailed regulations on *urban renewal and new development in yet undeveloped areas* (*Entwicklungsmassnahmen, Erneuerungsmassnahmen*). This weakness is due to the fact that state control of urban development falls within the competence of the Ministry of the Interior, and lawmakers of the Ministry of Environment and Regional Development did not want to intervene in the affairs of another department. Thus much is to be expected of, but little is known about, the ongoing work on the so-called *Municipal Act* in the Ministry of the Interior.

4.3   AMENDMENT OF URBAN PLANS

A *proliferation of plan amendments* was revealed by the case studies. At least two separate reasons have contributed to this: (1) a radical *shift in the actors and patterns of development* and (2) *excessively detailed plans* regulating elements even of minor importance.

In most cities the cumbersome work of producing a new plan or adapting the old ÁRTs and RRTs to changing circumstances usually was accompanied by fierce political battles in legislative boards. In some places these processes resulted in the reenactment of the "old" plan with minor changes (Balatonboglár) with the firm belief that *a well-regulated local system of zoning amendments* is an integral and rather useful part of planning. An excessive approach to making the planning process more adaptive to changing circumstances has been that zoning amendments are drafted by an in-house planner of the mayor's office (Kecskemét) *as part of the public service provision functions* of the city.

Specific "task forces" of cities (in most cases, comprised of the mayor or a deputy mayor, the heads of the public properties department and of the technical department, the chief architect, and in smaller municipalities the leader of the building authority, etc.) managing urban development tend to handle physical planning and zoning as an unavoidable but insignificant—even obstructive—mechanism and instruct the chief planner (Tatabánya) to commence preparations for zoning amendments if prevailing ordinances block desired developments.

In most municipalities studied there has been a manifest effort to redesign physical plans in such a manner that *they can function effectively as zoning plans*—i.e., land subdivision and building permits can be issued based on a single regulatory plan. Especially in those cities where "old" and "new" RRTs (detailed plans) have been integrated into the general plan (Kecskemét) this could result in an *overspecification of regulations* that may be in conflict with some minor parameters of an intended project.

As in 1991 the Constitutional Court came to the decision that all local planning measures must take the *legal form of a municipal statute*; plan amendment procedures are *regulated thoroughly* in the preamble of the statute of the general plan (ÁRT) in all cities studied. With some variations, the most commonly used procedure is as follows.

1. The planning commission *submits the proposal* for a zoning amendment to the legislative board.
2. The legislative board *comes to a decision*; if approval is given, the mayor's office *contacts public agencies* (and public utility companies) and authorities for their expert opinion or consent.
3. A *public hearing* is held.
4. The *opinion of the ministry* is solicited.
5. The legislative board *enacts the zoning amendment* in a municipal statute.

Provisions included in the 1997 act have been taken into account in most municipal statutes regulating the procedures for zoning amendments. According to some calculations the accomplishment of such a "legally valid" procedure of zoning amendment would take at least half a year. More than twenty-five agencies and authorities are involved. About one month is calculated for the completion of all steps if all actors comply within the time limits set by law.

Despite the definite will of ministerial lawmakers this type of procedure *functions as a planning permit*, which was not made part of the planning mechanism in Hungary by the 1997 act. Excluding only one city studied (Kecskemét, where the municipality tends to handle this process as part of public service provision), it is common that private developers pay for the plan amendment. In one of the cities studied (Eger), the office of the chief architect and the developer enter a contract: by signing a special form the developer accepts that the *chief architect's office is authorized to hire a mutually acceptable consultant planner* and that the *developer is charged a "management fee"* for the work of the office. The contract between the office and the developer also includes what proportion of the *fee paid to the consultant planner is to be covered by the developer* and what amount is to be paid as security to the municipality in advance.

4.4   VARIANCE PERMITS

Few of the above described plan amendment procedures have been declared by county administrative offices as "illegal." It is a definite hope that municipal innovations concerning variance permits also will stand the test of legality. This procedure has been introduced in some cities (Eger, Tatabánya) if *a regulation affects an owner in an inequitable manner or causes "unnecessary hardship"*—e.g., the zoning ordinance allows a maximum thirty percent land coverage index, while the existing index is forty percent, and the owner applies for a permit for the renewal (rebuilding) of a wing of his or her house. The procedure used in Eger is as follows.

1. The building authority informs the applicant that a precondition for the issuance of the requested permit is obtaining a variance permit.

2. The chief architect is consulted who, if he or she agrees, submits a proposal to the planning (in Eger, "urbanistic") committee.

3. The committee submits the proposal to the legislative board (in Eger, to the general assembly) that, if agreed, comes to an assembly (not administrative) decision.

4. The mayor signs the document, which then becomes the basis for the forthcoming administrative permit procedure performed by the building authority.

The county administrative offices have tested local innovations on variance permits as well. As all planning issues fall under the authority of the municipal legislative board (general assembly) only *those procedures have been suppressed that would have "ended" on the level of the planning committee* (despite this basic principle, in Tatabánya "less important" decisions on variances end with the committee).

Concerning variance permits there has been a definite fear of increasing the platforms at which *fraud and corruption* can occur. The opposite seems to be true (at least in Eger): if the process is well regulated locally and the highest levels of local decision making are involved, the danger of corruption can be reduced substantially.

4.5 NEGOTIATIONS AND "PLANNING GAINS"

This concept refers to the British practice of "planning permit." In the U.K. municipalities can obtain some dedications from developers in land, or improvements in the course of a discretionary procedure of planning permit. Although *law in Hungary has introduced no such procedures,* municipalities are rather active in obtaining some "gains" when developers apply for amendment to the plans. According to Central European planning traditions, *developers and owners do not possess the right to submit official claims for zoning amendments.*

Special negotiations concerning dedications usually occur before cities enact plan amendments—i.e., in the course of plan making by consultant or in-house planners and when these "official" zoning plans are discussed officially or semi-officially by the mayor, deputy mayors, responsible city officials, the chief architect, the planning commission, etc. In most cases dedications are obtained in

the form of land or improvements rather than in money, as noted in the example of Balatonboglár.

In a city on Lake Balaton new owners of a large tract that previously was a camping site wanted to split the lot into smaller building sites, because demand on the lakefront increased for small plots and decreased for large ones; thus, such subdivision was more profitable. In the course of the plan amendment process the planning commission and the legislative board discussed the requests many times and thoroughly examined various solutions. As the site was undeveloped and landscaped the city decided to avoid intensive development and agreed that a fifteen meter-wide strip of public land would "be planned" along the shore. The same was agreed in another place, where a narrow street providing access to the lake was set as a condition for land subdivision (though it is not yet settled whether the city will pay for the public lands or will acquire them at no cost).

These and similar practices raise the question *if "contract zoning" can be considered "legal"*—i.e., if a legislative process of plan amendment might be connected to a contract of civil law between the municipality and the developer. Although some lawyers, after consulting the Constitutional Court, claim that the legal institution of a "municipal contract" is required, ministerial officials (those who worked on the 1997 act) are against any such kind of bargaining. They recommend utilization of *bonuses* as an adequate mechanism for solving the problem of planning gains: precisely set ordinances and standards are to be formulated in the regulatory plan indicating the conditions under which the municipality is entitled to obtain gains and what allowances are to be provided to the developer as a consequence. The legal problems of planning gains have not yet emerged more seriously because in the majority of cases bargaining took place when public, municipally owned land was sold for development.

There are many variations in the cities and villages studied concerning how local bodies and officials cooperate in urban physical planning and development. Institutional settings and methods of cooperation largely depend on the size of the municipality. In small cities and villages, cooperation is less formal; responsibilities formally are fixed, but actual activities tend to overstep institutional boundaries. In large cities a more definite separation among public actors is characteristic, and in many places this separation gives way to special governmental bodies or task forces.

5 Planning and Environmental Control

A special environmentalist attitude to urban planning has evolved in Hungary since the second half of the 1980s. This is manifested both in a conservationist approach and in land use planning less focused on functional segregation. Parallel to the international trends that lead supporters of both approaches, architect-planners back the preservation of urban heritage and mixed-use development. They argue that in order to establish and preserve "functionally rich" urban environments all types of land uses may, in theory, coexist if specific emissions and immissions of nuisances are below predetermined levels and are effectively controlled. This attitude is reflected in the title of the 1997 act (Formation and Protection of Built Environment) and even more strongly in OTÉK, which prescribes that regulatory plans *shall set emission and immission standards for all zoning categories.* Lawmakers, however, have not been fully aware of the important adverse effects of this regulatory mechanism.

5.1 PARTIAL INTEGRATION OF ENVIRONMENTAL CONTROL INTO PLANNING

International (European and American) trends demonstrate an effort towards a more comprehensive manner of environmental control in cities: basic urban physical plans are subject to "generic" *environmental impact studies* or "statements" (e.g., EIS in New York State) instead of direct integration of some elements of environmental control into land use planning and zoning. Moreover, it is almost *impossible to attach correct environmental standards to land use categories* or to zoning districts, especially concerning noise, vibration levels and air pollution.

In the late 1970s rigorous standards were introduced in Hungary by the responsible ministries referring to the *permitted levels of pollution "in the surroundings" of* (not within) *specific structures and land use categories* (e.g., "high density residential areas," "mixed use areas"). These standards rarely have been used in urban plans and have never succeeded in establishing real conformity with land use, zoning and categories.

The latter problem refers to the very complicated nature of specific environmental pollution to be controlled (e.g.,

in the back garden of a long residential building overlooking a major road, noise levels may be substantially lower than on the other side, which is exposed to heavy traffic; levels of air pollution in a specific area also are influenced by nonlocal, remote factors). Provisions in OTÉK prescribing that emission and immission standards be attached to zoning categories cannot be realized at this moment; if environmental standards are included in binding plans and ordinances, no building permits would be possible for residential structures in the central parts of cities.

The specific institutional position and procedures of environmental control may cause even more serious problems. As discussed in more detail in section 4, special purpose authorities have two tasks in the course of urban development: to review urban plans and to give consent to specific urban projects permitted in most cases by the building authorities. While their findings concerning urban plans are not binding to municipalities, many building permits may be issued only if their consent has been granted (in other words, they serve in an advisory capacity concerning urban plans but may make a final decision concerning specific projects). One example from Budapest shows that this institutional setting may curtail substantially the planning powers of municipalities.

For about fifteen years the widening of a road that would connect two motorways to the third ring road of Budapest through a new bridge across the Danube has been planned. Naturally, the city's general plan (ÁRT) included this scheme. By enacting the ÁRT, the general assembly also accepted the widening of the street, which would relieve the downtown of some through-traffic, but for a length of four hundred meters would have run between residential buildings. A compensation scheme was offered by the city to homeowners adversely affected by the nuisance of the increased traffic after local inhabitants protested against the project.

The street widening fell under the requirement for an environmental impact study (which will be reviewed later). The study was prepared in great detail by leading experts and showed that by specific mitigation measures adverse effects could be lessened substantially and that in

43

other parts of the city positive environmental impacts would result, offsetting many of the negative impacts on the site. The city applied for building permits step-by-step as implementation of the project proceeded.

A majority of the work was accomplished and most compensation payments were made when the regional office of the National Health and Medical Officer (as a special purpose authority) refused to give consent for the final phase of the project. If this decision is not changed Budapest's newest bridge will continue to have extremely poor and complicated access from both the city and from the international road network, and the main goal of relieving the downtown area from extreme traffic burdens will not be achieved.

5.2   ENVIRONMENTAL IMPACT STUDIES

Urban physical plans must have a *section on environmental protection and control* supplementary to the map of the regulatory plan and to the zoning ordinance. Only those elements of the environmental section of the plan included in the latter two documents are binding. In addition to these planning provisions an EIS must be prepared for major projects listed in an appendix of a 1995 government statute issued as a bylaw to the *1995 Act on the Protection of the Environment.*

A majority of projects requiring EIS are related to agriculture, manufacturing, mining, water management, urban infrastructure, waste disposal and waste management. The EIS requirement refers to *newly established plants and activities* and to those activities for which the *volume is enlarged by twenty-five percent* compared to their former (permitted) volume. For some plants and activities *a threshold limit* is included in the law indicating the size of the activity under which no EIS is required: e.g., oil refinery—fifteen thousand tons per year, dyes—five thousand tons per year, extraction from ground water—one thousand cubic meters per day, sewage plants—five thousand cubic meters per day. In 1997 some new activities were included in the statute: *shopping centers with more than twenty thousand net square meters* of floorspace and (besides motorways and first and second rank national roads) all *local roads* that interconnect national and international roads within cities and/or *carry traffic heavier than one thousand eight hundred standard units per day.*

In Hungary the EIS is attached as background material to applications for *environmental permits.* The permitting authority is the regional office of the *Inspectorate of the Environment.* The 1997 government statute gives a list of other authorities and agencies that *should be contacted* as *special purpose authorities*: e.g., Directorate of Nature Conservation or directorate of the affected natural park, regional office of the National Health and Medical Officer, the affected forestry inspectorate, the Geological Service, the regional office of the Directorate of Water Management, the notary and/or the building authority of the affected municipality, etc. Contacting a great number of other agencies and authorities might be required, which is left to the discretion of the inspectorate: e.g., Hungarian Office of Mining, Hungarian Agency of Energy, Inspectorate of Telecommunications, Directorate for Air, National Meteorological Service, etc.

The issuance of an environmental permit is a rather complicated and time-consuming activity in Hungary. In order to both accelerate the process and to ensure thorough review of the application *a preliminary and a detailed EIS* are now mandatory due to the 1995 act. Similar to the U.S. system, which is based on a preliminary EIS, the inspectorate can:

- cease the procedure after finding that the activity does not fall under the requirements for an environmental permit (and for the EIS);
- grant the permit if the contents of the preliminary EIS are acceptable;
- decide whether or not a second, detailed EIS is necessary;
- refuse the request for a permit.

If the preliminary permit is not refused, the inspectorate notifies the notary of the affected municipality, which is obliged to publicize the decision of the inspectorate. If the applicant is required to hand in a second, detailed EIS, the inspectorate may consider the findings of the general public. It is recommended by government statute that the *central aim of the preliminary procedure is to select among* the possible *alternatives.* The inspectorate is bound to make a preliminary selection.

5.3   "GREENS" STRENGTHENED

As seen from the above description of the EIS, the 1995 Act on the Environment and the related government statute tended to focus preliminarily on some "environmentally sensible" sectors of industry and services. Provisions concerning important urban elements, like shopping centers and local roads, were a direct reaction to the protests of affected citizens led by grass root environmentalist groups that later organized themselves into rather strong associations. In Budapest the "Working Group on Air" is the best-organized "green" group.

These associations oppose the construction of motorways and new metro lines and try to block new developments in the inner city, even in cases such as former industrial sites that are slated for conversion into urban parks. This attitude is relatively strong among members of the local councils and also in the central government. In some cases, such as in downtown Budapest, they may thwart needed redevelopment and renewal projects.

5.4 ENVIRONMENTAL AND PLANNING CONTROL OF SHOPPING MALLS IN BUDAPEST

In Budapest libertarian, free market and environmentalist attitudes have collided concerning shopping malls in recent years. The noninterventionist approach is backed by the fact that "progrowth" municipalities in the metropolitan region have introduced no regulations; thus, strict regulation within the city would have resulted in an unfavorable concentration of malls in the urban fringe along motorways without adequate public transport access. In August 1998 a rather rigorous and complicated regulatory mechanism in the framework regulatory plan and ordinance was accepted by the general assembly of the city. The main regulatory elements are the following:

- for all shopping facilities exceeding six thousand square meters a *district regulatory plan* (KSzT) must be established; in addition, an urban planning impact study, an impact study on retailing, a complex environmental impact study, a study on impacts on traffic and a study of the cityscape are required;
- in the inner city the maximum permitted gross floorspace of shopping facilities is twenty thousand square meters (in inner Buda, only fifteen thousand);
- for shopping facilities exceeding the above size a "permit for rezoning" is required (a special "floating" zone is included in the ordinance; i.e., the zoning district is not mapped, but it is defined above which area of the city the zone may "float"), but the size of the shopping facility may not, without "bonuses," exceed thirty-five thousand square meters anywhere.

These regulations came into force in January 1999. The strict size limit of thirty-five thousand square meters is explained by the fact that decision-makers have been convinced that the already established shopping centers and those under construction or in the process of obtaining building permits would "more than satisfy" these requirements (many applications were submitted for shopping center building permits in response to the prospect of tightened regulations).

For new shopping centers above twenty thousand square meters designated as special zones as described above, a specific "zonal" regulation has been introduced. Two important location preferences have been taken into account: areas close to metro stations and locations in the transitional zone (the area between the inner city and the 1872 border of Budapest, where manufacturing activities are in sharp decline). If a shopping facility is planned within three hundred meters from a metro station or one thousand meters from a tram station or railway line, a five thousand square meter "floorspace bonus" is given above the determined limit.

In specific areas of the transitional zone, thirty thousand—and in other parts, thirty-five thousand—square meters are permitted without bonuses, while in zones closer to the center, twenty thousand—and in the outer zone (beyond the 1872 border of the city), twenty-five thousand—square meters is the permitted maximum without bonuses. Control of aesthetics, landscaping and parking is also rather rigorous: in some zones the permitted number of parking lots is reduced to the nationally regulated maximum, part (usually one-third) of the parking lots must be constructed in the basement of the structure, parking lots must be landscaped (one tree for every four parking spaces), one-third of the prescribed—landscaped—open space must be maintained as one single unit, etc.

This regulatory framework corresponds to its counterparts in many European countries. It is hard to say, however, whether it was adopted in time or too late. Thorough studies about the actual impact on the total retail sector of the city are yet to be undertaken.

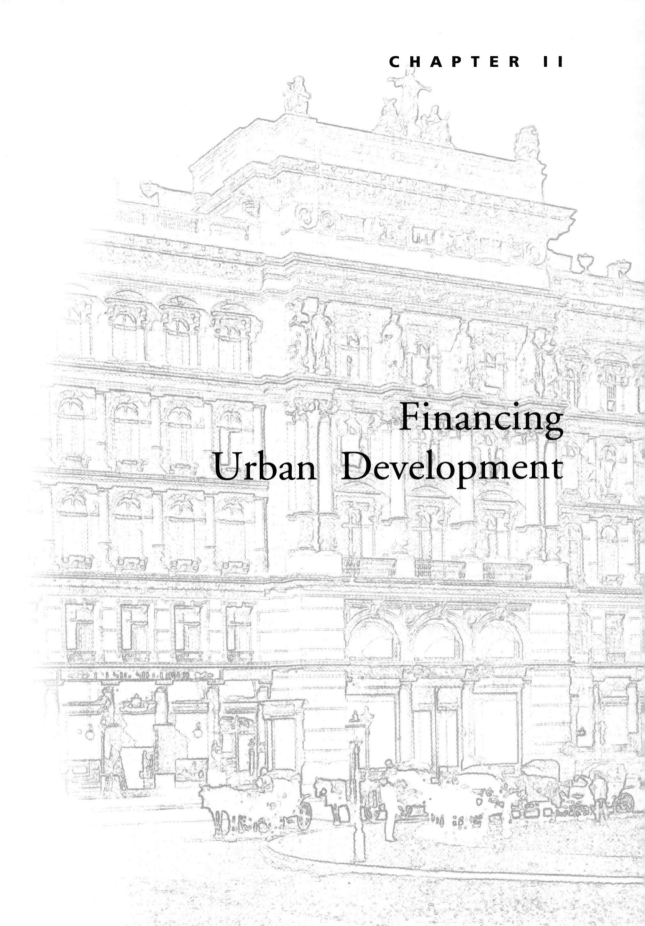

Financing
Urban Development

URBAN PLANNING AND CAPITAL INVESTMENT FINANCING IN HUNGARY

1 Planning Process

This chapter examines the methodological issues of urban development as well as the potential for development and local financial management using both a general and a specific approach. Urban planning and, obviously, urban development are *forward-looking* activities that analyze current conditions and outline a vision as well as one or more versions of its implementation.

1.1 METHODOLOGICAL APPROACH

In terms of methodology, a key *conclusion* drawn from the case studies is that the technical design and economic development work phases of urban planning are prepared utilizing various *methods*. Different methodologies are used for technical and economic community planning, which gives rise to a number of conflicts. It goes without saying that neither technical nor economic urban planning are accomplished without specific data sets, but the two approaches use them differently in the planning process.

Technical planning prepares *factual, "reliably measurable"* plans from the data sets (meters, square meters, kilowatts, demographic indicators, number of apartments, etc.), including urban development with technical content (capacity expansion or reduction). Economic planning can generate *"unreliable"* plans from the available— calculated and collected—data that can be used only with *a certain degree of probability* (budgeted revenues and expenditures, expected yields, potential market costs and benefits, estimated changes in property values, etc.).

The preparation of *civic design plans* (master plans) cannot be separated from the economic approach or, in other words, the objectives of the persons preparing and implementing the plans (principal, implementer, user, subject, etc.). Even though intentions may be driven by technical considerations, the idea of the preparation of a new urban plan fundamentally is socially driven, as it attempts to resolve the existential issues of the community concerned that exist in the present but affect the future.

The original intention of the principal is to create a regulated future derived from the present as altered by internal and external factors. The objective of planners cannot be anything but to formulate better, cleaner, more manageable "interest force fields" by plans.

The economic work phases of *urban development plans* also are permeated by this approach. Therefore, the attitude of economic planners is driven by the need to ensure the increase of current living standards or—more specifically—of economic output or, if this is already achieved, the sustainability of harmonic economic growth. This must be based on analysis of existing economic trends, which can be described accurately but can forecast future effects only "unreliably," because economic processes and their effects cannot be planned with the precision of a technical design.

Thus, the underlying motive of the two kinds of planning is identical. The view taken here is that the problem lies in the failure to coordinate the technical work of the two types of urban planning efforts. Despite the different genres, this could be achieved if city management prepares medium- and long-term *development strategy plans*. Currently city managers do not do so or do not place great emphasis on them, as they do not consider them to be true "scenarios." Here the term urban development is understood to mean general—economic, cultural, technical and infrastructural—development; that is, it is not applied only to local economy and municipal finances (this definition will be elaborated in the "Strategic Planning" section). For the remainder of this study, concentration will rest on urban planning from the economic approach.

1.2 ECONOMIC APPROACH

The main issue concerning this approach is which footholds and starting points can be identified in the planning of an uncertain economic future. In the current, short- and medium-term economic environment in Hungary the fundamental motivation is the *necessity for capital accumulation and capital raising*. After all, this ensures the feasibility of urban development plans and support of the participants concerned. Accordingly, the economic aspects of urban development must *serve the purposes of planning for local economic growth* (engendering, maintaining, harmonizing, curbing, etc.) *and analyzing the potential for growth.*

Local economic growth means the *relative maximization (optimization) of the quality of life of residents and the earnings and wealth generation potential of local economic actors* in the environment and planning period concerned. This includes human services (social effects) and the issue of the use of the environment.

1.2.1 Constraints

What are the fundamental national economy constraints currently and in the medium and long term (from five to fifteen years) on local economic processes and on municipal financial management? What are the constraints that every community faces?

Here, the following points are assumed.

- Central government funds, one of the traditional resources of local economic processes, have been shrinking for years; they are not expected to grow even in the medium term.

- Municipalities sold most of their marketable assets. This resulted in the depletion of property because municipalities did not use such resources as capital; that is, they did not reinvest the proceeds in the local economy.

- Under the current circumstances the taxpaying or tax-bearing capacity of local economic organizations and residents is highly limited. Necessary economic growth could be initiated and/or sustained through the alleviation of tax and social insurance contribution burdens; furthermore, the local tax system must be redesigned so that it offers incentives and is differentiated according to value rather than serving a punitive role.

1.2.2 Competitive Environment, Competitive Position

Among national economy constraints potential changes in the local economic force field must be identified and forecasted. Such changes also affect the competitive position of economic actors in the community concerned. Competitiveness should be interpreted in the context of exploiting local economic resources and potential and launching or sustaining economic growth. In general, only producing competitive products or providing competitive services can ensure economic growth; the basis for this is to ensure necessary conditions in terms of *infrastructure and information as well as a proentrepreneurial environment.*

Accessibility, reliability and knowledge (skills, innovative character, etc.) are crucial in terms of the geographical aspects of competitiveness; infrastructural factors are closely related to these. Civic design master plans establish and regulate the infrastructural technical-physical framework in the broadest sense possible, which also affects competitiveness. Thus, comprehensive, strategically sound urban development plans must take into consideration natural resources (mineral deposits, water reserves, economic geographic factors, tourist facilities, etc.) and social characteristics (demography, labor structure, education, health care, cultural traditions, etc.) of the region concerned.

For purposes of urban development it is assumed that the state will be unable to support substantially more regional, microregional or macroregional infrastructural projects. Funding for local infrastructural development can be generated only by the economic growth, capital raising and retention capabilities of the region concerned.

Paradoxically, the expected growth of infrastructural projects on a national scale and with central government participation may be detrimental to individual communities. This is because to achieve European Union (EU) accession the government must press primarily for macroregional infrastructural systems, the local effects of which probably will be much tougher, as they are designed for economic and geographical considerations on a European scale.

The construction or altered route of a motorway or high speed railway line may increase or decrease the economic area of a microregion by orders of magnitude. Consider, for instance, the impact of frequent changes in the planned locations of bridges of geographical and structural significance, the rearrangement of time schedules for construction, conceptual controversies about the regulation of large river systems and hydroelectric plants.

The EU also supports the rapid establishment of large, macroregional infrastructures, obviously in light of continental European economic and political interests. This is further complicated by the "flexible" behavior of international private capital, which has an increasing role in implementation, and by the "inflexibility" of the concession procedure, which "sets the future in stone."

1.3 CONTENT OF URBAN DEVELOPMENT

1.3.1 General

The implementation of an urban development plan represents interference in the socioeconomic processes. Thus, the changes prompted by the urban development concept and program objectives, whether existing or in the pipeline, to the economy of the community concerned must be examined. In other words, analysis involves the quantitative and qualitative opportunities and constraints to be considered in the existing economic structure. On the other hand, the feasibility of implementation requires consideration, as the plan also addresses local household and political interests. Therefore, the plan must strive to achieve an optimum compromise. Any intervention, including civic design and development plans, will jeopardize interests and introduce bias.

In this study the examination and evaluation of changes in the economic potential of communities and the formulation of recommendations based on the conclusions is a fundamental methodological issue.

1.3.2 Specific

Regarding the specific economic approach, the key issues are: which new processes will be engendered by the plan in the community concerned, and what effects will it have on the economic potential of the community? More specifically, to what extent will the future plan affect, positively (improvement) or negatively (tension generation), the market position (development, investment, etc.) of economic units operating or wanting to settle in the community and its economic structure?

Positive effects include improved living standards, profit margins, employment, purchasing power, tax potential—in short: economic growth. Negative effects are the opposite: a narrowing of the economic force field and the necessity for crisis management programs. The outcome of the examination of positive and negative effects (SWOT analysis—Strengths, Weaknesses, Opportunities) is the basis for *compromise* between the two genres and for *common strategic planning*. In the final analysis, the objective of planners and principals is to coordinate such economic and social effects to achieve a positive, dynamic equilibrium.

The aforementioned economic entities include municipalities and their economic or regional-federal organizations. Municipalities play a major role in the economy of communities. On the one hand, they pursue *economic and regional development* activities, and on the other, they perform *economic organization* tasks because they have the power to influence the local and regional economic environment (local tax and wage policy, real estate management, development of regional and urban development strategies, infrastructural development, issuance of construction and operating permits, etc.).

Thus, municipalities and regional development companies as well as associations of municipalities participate on both the supply and the demand sides of the economy. Let us consider *which tasks civic design plans* (development master plans) *impose on local economic management* (decision-makers, beneficiaries, implementers, etc.), which may include:

- mandatory sewage network management;
- construction bans in certain locations, as a result of which construction or industrial sites must be identified and improved elsewhere at extra cost;
- property value fluctuations;
- changes in financial expenses (e.g., transportation, commuting);
- technological quality requirements, as a result of which some businesses in the community may become profitable or loss making;
- changes in business opportunities and the conditions of opening sites that affect local tax and real estate policy, housing structure, living standards, employment and thus the urban and regional development potential of municipalities;
- restriction on the urban development in one community while increasing the potential of others due to the exploitation of regional resources that are concent-rated in certain areas (e.g., resort development, establishment of industrial parks, new commercial and service functions resulting from the rearrangement of traffic patterns, residential development);
- preparation of new master and specific development plans.

The key issue is that in the present the plan appears to the parties concerned as an external factor imposed on them from above. Therefore, urban development plans, irrespective of their scale, may force local and regional actors, municipalities or their associations to *change strategies*. As a strong social effect, this situation engenders conflict and may lead to the dramatic stalemate of the NIMBYsyndrome ("not in my back yard" = I am all for development and change as long as it is not in my direct vicinity).

1.3.3 Cost Calculation

Accordingly, the need to *determine the cost* of changes also arises, which is a very complex and risky task. An attempt must be made to express the economic effect of master plans and development plans in cash terms. The most simple and immediate effect, for instance, is the increase or reduction in the value of certain areas where real property values change significantly—increasing, stagnating or decreasing—thus altering the future conditions of earning a living.

One methodological issue is finding a way to handle the shift among economic, social and environmental effects, which may prompt different responses from residents, entrepreneurs and politicians in the short, medium and long term. Furthermore, environmental effects must be regulated through urban planning means; in other words, such effects are built into regulatory plans. The following questions arise: Is it possible to regulate expected economic and social effects? How can all this be measured? Which indicators must be systematized to estimate these processes and their results?

1.3.4 Information and Monitoring System

The current local planning system and the statistical system based on it are appropriate only for analyzing the past. Under present conditions analyzing the past and extrapolating trends is not enough. A different type of thinking is required; implementation has become the fundamental issue.

Impact assessment must be based not only on the analysis of problems and conflicts but also on the *identification of values*. Impact assessment including the identification of values would make the planning process orderly, forward-looking and thus realistic. There are always fewer values and resources than problems. Therefore, in addition to problem analysis, it is necessary to analyze values as well (problem map + value map).

The information and monitoring system of the effects of urban development plans and projects must have access to the following data sets:

- information related to business conditions in the various economic sectors;
- information related to real property and to the market value of property;
- municipal, regional and county budgets;
- centrally earmarked and other domestic and international funding;
- data pertaining to local purchasing power;
- market research data.

It is beneficial to maintain a cadastre-type register of local and regional values—economic, cultural, architectural, environmental, etc. The creation, operation and maintenance of the value cadastre and service provisions based on it (such as marketing policy) are the key roles of the users of the future plan.

The objective of this section is to promote, through economic data, the measuring and planning of local economic trends and thus the calculation of economic growth or decline. In Hungary this is not as sophisticated as financial information and the budgeting system of manufacturing or commercial enterprises.

Existing and systematized data must serve as the starting point. The following sources may be considered for the systematizing of municipal financial management data:

- Central Statistical Office publications (Hungarian acronym: TSTAR);
- data and classifications of the publication entitled "The key financial and coverage indicators of municipalities and their property cadastre data" compiled by the Ministry of the Interior with the help of the county Regional Administrative, Fiscal Information Service (TÁKISZ), the metropolitan FÁKISZ and the information technology service of the National Tax Office (APEH-SzTADI);
- data series compiled independently by municipalities, regional associations and development companies.

The latter are particularly important data sources because the independence of municipalities necessarily leads to the evolution of data classifications reflecting local conditions. The experience of planners shows that the center and the municipalities think and plan in different ways. The situation is akin to the phenomenon in which two companies in similar lines of business pursue different philosophies and management systems even though their objectives are identical—namely, to produce as much profit as possible under specific conditions, within a given timeframe and in view of existing economic partners and competitors. Thus, the information basis, in order to be realistic, should contain central as well as municipal data classifications.

1.3.5 Value Map

An important element of this concept is that the existing *municipal property cadastre must be extended to nonmunicipal real property*, because the municipality is not the only entity to own property, the future of properties with various forms of ownership is interrelated, and the economy of the community greatly depends on changes in the real estate market. A comprehensive property cadastre may provide continuous information on technical parameters as well as ownership structures and property value changes in the community. Without this it is impossible to pursue a realistic regional development and municipal property policy or to prepare a realistic master development plan.

In the future the property cadastre may be the basis for the gradual expansion of the *local tax and fee system* controlled by local citizens, which presumably will play a much greater role in the future than it does today. The expansion of local taxes and duties is highly important; if these provided the main funding sources for the maintenance and expansion of urban public services, a close relationship among revenues, wealth and the quality of public services would be created. Not only would the municipality obtain additional funding, but demand and accountability would increase.

The implementation of this easy formula is questionable in the short term, since today no further tax burdens or fee increases may be imposed on citizens and economic organizations. At the same time it is obvious that the central budget will not give up its tax, contribution and fee revenues in the near future, which could—and should—be reallocated to the municipalities (decentralized), whereby *the proportion of self-generated revenues would increase within the local budget without the imposition of additional burdens to the community*. In perspective all this means is that local revenues can be increased from the accumulation of wealth, raising internal or external capital (including borrowing, securities and concession-based arrangements) and local tax and fee income. It seems appropriate that the majority of locally generated or locally concentrated funds that are not needed to finance operations and maintenance be allocated to *urban development fund(s)*.

The revenues of these funds would come from the proceeds of privatized real property, a proportion of taxes and fees, borrowing, domestic and foreign funds distributed though tendering procedures and the issue of securities. Expenditures would be spent on infrastructural development, the improvement of public services, the improvement of public spaces, indirect developments promoting the increase of property value, etc. The key to the operation of the funds would be to reinvest a specified part of revenues into the development of public services and infrastructure. Local revenues would generate public property and general growth in wealth.

1.4 STRATEGIC PLANNING

Urban development means development of social and economic resources, quality of the environment and technical facilities of a community that creates balanced conditions for economic growth and improved living standards. Starting from the general economic climate today, the following requirements apply to urban development:

- *a competitive position*—the capital required for development places municipalities in a market position;
- *flexibility*—adaptability to the ever-changing domestic and international socioeconomic conditions, effects and trends is required;
- *participation*—the definition of goals and the activities necessary to achieve them with the involvement of the broader community are necessary for efficient development.

The fundamental methodological content of the preparation of an urban development plan includes:

- *definition of the community*—economic, physical and intellectual resources and conditions;
- *feedback coordination*—relating available resources and conditions to desires and possibilities and formulation of opinion on the local level;
- *tools and timing of implementation*;
- *regulatory procedures.*

The scenario of the preparation of the urban development plan follows:

- *investigation, identification of resources*;
- coordination;
- *program, development of concept*;
- coordination;
- *preparation of plan*;

- coordination;
- *legitimization procedure (decree, resolution).*

It is recommended that preparation of the strategy be split into the following work phases.

1. *Identification of objectives*—delimitation of the preparatory (investigation), proposal (concept and program) and implementation (business plan) phases in terms of content, structure and timing, involving:
   - identification of priorities;
   - creation of a database;
   - preparation of a real estate value map;
   - identification of task groups;
   - model of municipal financial management (taxes, rents, property management, other financial provisions);
   - "wealth generating wealth" program (financial-organizational model);
   - time schedule for the preparation of plan, deadlines;
   followed by feedback and coordination.

2. *Preparation (investigation, identification of resources),* including:
   - interpretation of national and county regional development concepts on the regional and municipal levels;
   - EU integration, Phare programs;
   - analysis of relationships with county and other communities in the agglomeration and adjacent regions;
   - analysis of the economy of the community (population, sectors, economic organization, local wealth and income structure, etc.);
   - review of the financial management of the municipality (budget, property management, involvement of external funds);
   - review of real property values (identification of price-value zones);
   - review of ownership relations;
   - review of interests (chambers, nongovernmental organizations, local politics, etc.);
   - role of the preservation of values as a development factor;
   - business effects of the master plans in force;
   - review of documents in force pertaining to urban development;
   - economic effects of education, cultural activities; identification of the community's human resources and assessment of potential;
   - housing estates (floating plots, renovation, etc.);

- preliminary identification of funding sources (central government and other external funds, both private and institutional);
followed by feedback, coordination and identification of funds I.

3. *Proposal (concept and program),* including:
   - definition of strategic directions;
   - concept design;
   - conditions of launching the process of increasing the value of areas;
   - model of municipal financial management (taxes, rents, property management, other financial provisions);
   - "wealth generating wealth" program (financial-organizational model);
   - linkages with master development plans;
   - identification of new construction sites (residential, industrial, commercial and resort zones);
   - identification of reserve zones;
   - linkages to other financial plans of the municipality;
   - development of system of preferences;
   - involvement of household funds;
   - elaboration of system of incentives for economic organizations;
   - raising external funds;
   - relationship of parts of the community;
   followed by feedback, coordination and identification of funds II.

4. *Implementation (business plan),* including:
   - elaboration of urban development alternatives in terms of time, function, funding;
   - modeling the relationship of the community, its parts and communities in agglomeration;
   - implementation plan of real property management;
   - "commissioning plan" of real estate value map;
   - organization of real estate supply, real estate exchange;
   - community marketing;
   followed by the legitimization process (decree, resolution).

1.5 SOCIAL AND ECONOMIC IMPACT ASSESSMENT

In the work phases of assessment and program design, data and indicators must reflect the initial situation and relationships: that is, local economic conditions, potential and internal interrelations.

1.5.1 Social Impacts

Indicators of social impacts include:
- demographic data;
- labor structure and employment;
- migration;
- problem map and conflict potential;
- survey based on sociological and opinion poll methods concerning expectations about changes in place of residence, employment and environment (ideas, intentions, expectations, etc.);
- data from cost of living calculations;
- assessment of the conflicts of interest generated by the master plan or expected to arise, based on sociological methods.

1.5.2 Economic Impacts

Indicators of economic impacts include:
- ownership structure;
- cadastre of real property downtown and in the outskirts, based on market value;
- area use balance;
- real estate market data and trends;
- local GDP figures;
- credit and mortgage terms;
- quantifiable data of sectoral and regional development concepts;
- data on economic organizations;
- municipal financial management and budget data;
- local taxes, rent and usage fees;
- central earmarked funds;
- enumeration of various domestic and international funds available through tendering;
- business and household tax figures, taxation terms;
- wage trends;
- infrastructural coverage and capacity data;
- cost of public utility use;
- operating data of institutions related to basic services;
- data related to the protection of the environment;
- tourism data.

The information and monitoring system also must contain data concerning *local purchasing power, local capital concentration* (potential wealth, working capital, market value of fixed assets, etc.) and *local (county, microregion level) GDP*, which are needed to examine and plan economic processes realistically. Such data include:
- price indices;
- wage indices;
- real wage calculations;
- profitability indicators and rates of return;
- credit and deposit portfolios;
- interest rate changes.

1.5.3 An Example

Below are some examples for the economic component of the information system. The example is for purposes of illustration only; therefore, the system may be more comprehensive or may utilize a different structure. The frequency of data collection indicated here is annual, though higher frequency can be ensured for some data. The year 1990 was selected, when the market economy and thus the analysis and planning of realistic economic trends were introduced.

Budget

For a description of the budgetary components of municipal information systems, see table 4.

Other financial assets

This data set contains the domestic and foreign funds available to communities, counties and microregions. The grouping is useful for financial planning, external capital raising and the assessment of completed projects. The data include information currently available on the value of real estate, because such changes are the best indicators of the evolution of the economic trends in a given community, be they the effects of infrastructural development or of the income structure of the household or business sectors. The data on real estate values must be refined, which hopefully will happen upon the modernization of property registration (land registry offices, municipal property cadastres, etc.).

The information base should be broken down into more *subgroups*, because the various budget items, domestic and foreign funds involve different terms—priorities (e.g., industrial parks, environmental protection), concessions (e.g., local or central taxation), exemptions, self-generated funding (e.g., grants, Phare programs), repayment terms, etc. It is a fundamental technical requirement that maps and graphic work (graphs, tables, etc.) be attached to impact assessments.

For a description of the budgetary components of municipal information systems, see table 5.

Table 4
Budgetary Components of Municipal Information Systems

Data Group:	Financial Assets	Data Subgroup 1:	Budget
Frequency:	Annual	Starting Year:	1990
Data Source:	Central, county, municipal budgets, legal regulations, official journals		

DATA	REFERENCE UNIT		
	Community	County	Region
Revenues [total]	X	X	X
Central Grants [total]	X	X	X
Normative Grants	X	X	X
Earmarked and Targeted Subsidies	X		
Other Grants	X	X	X
Shared Central Taxes [total]	X	X	X
Personal Income Tax	X		
Personal Income Tax per Capita	X		
Motor Vehicle Tax	X		
Local Taxes and Duties [total]	X		
Land Tax	X		
Building Tax	X		
Communal Tax [businesses]	X		
Communal Tax [private persons]	X		
Business Tax	X		
Tourism Tax	X		
Income from Stamp Duties	X		
Property Management [total]	X		
Sale of Land	X	X	X
Sale of Housing	X	X	X
Sale of Nonresidential Real Estate	X	X	X
Rent and Usage Fees	X	X	X
Sale of Shares and Business Stakes	X	X	X
Dividends	X	X	X
Other Securities	X	X	
Financial Assets Transferred	X	X	X
Interest Income	X	X	X
Other Income	X	X	X
Value-added Tax	X	X	
Credit	X	X	X

Table 4 (continued)
Budgetary Components of Municipal Information Systems

DATA	REFERENCE UNIT		
	Community	County	Region
Expenditures [total]	X	X	X
Operating and Maintenance Expenditures	X	X	X
Renovation	X	X	X
Development	X	X	X
Accumulation of Funds	X	X	X
Housing Fund	X	X	
Infrastructural Fund	X	X	X
Social Fund	X	X	X
Miscellaneous	X	X	X
Reserve Generation	X	X	X
Other	X	X	X

Table 5
Financial Asset Components of Municipal Information Systems

Data Group:	Financial Assets	Data Subgroup 2:	Other Financial Assets
Frequency:	Annual	Starting Year:	1990
Data Source:	Central, county, regional, municipal budgets, legal regulations, official journals, publications		

DATA	REFERENCE UNIT		
	Community	County	Region
Central Funds [total]	X	X	X
Grants for Infrastructural Development	X	X	X
Grants to Businesses	X	X	X
Earmarked Funds [total]	X	X	X
Central Environmental Fund	X	X	X
Labor Market Fund	X	X	X
National Cultural Fund	X	X	X
Road Fund	X	X	X
Water Management Fund	X	X	X
Targeted Appropriations Managed by Ministries [total]	X	X	X
Ministry of Agriculture and Regional Development	X	X	X
Ministry of the Economy	X	X	X
Ministry of the Environment	X	X	X
Miscellaneous	X	X	X

Table 5 (continued)
Financial Asset Components of Municipal Information Systems

DATA	REFERENCE UNIT		
	Community	County	Region
International Funds [total]	X	X	X
Phare	X	X	X
EU Funds	X	X	X
Aid	X	X	X
Credit	X	X	X
Other Domestic Funds [total]	X	X	X
Foundations	X	X	X
Targeted Associations	X	X	X
Municipality-owned Property	X	X	X
Marketable	X	X	X
Limited Marketability	X	X	X
Unmarketable	X	X	X
Municipality-owned Real Estate	X	X	X
Book Value	X	X	X
Market Value	X	X	X
Nonmunicipality-owned Real Estate	X	X	X
Market Value	X	X	X
Concessions to Entrepreneurial Zones	X	X	X
Other Concessions	X	X	X

1.6 PROPERTY MANAGEMENT AND COMMUNITY PLANS

Municipalities also require a property management strategy in line with the master development plan. The timeframe of the master development plan is ten to fifteen years, but obviously one needs to look further ahead concerning certain issues, such as ring roads, bridge construction, railway development, technical infrastructure development, identification of residential and industrial zones, development needs of educational and health care institutions and environmental protection or concession (build-operate-transfer) agreements.

A long-term approach is a characteristic of this planning genre despite the fact that master development plans may be considered for review or modification after a few years. The aforementioned conflict between the approach of planners and that of local management also exists during the preparation of the master development plan concept and program design. The conflict in this case is that municipal officials must think in terms of the *four-year election cycle*, which is considerably shorter than the time-frame of the master development plan. Even the most ambitious and forward-looking managers and representatives may not think in terms of more than two election cycles; responsible planning is not possible for periods longer than that. Even so, daily experience and evolving economic and political conditions continually alter and reshuffle conceptions, which furthermore may change significantly after local elections. Moreover, after general elections new legislation and the new government may alter the existing operating conditions for the administration and financial management of municipalities. Planners, on the other hand, must analyze large-scale trends and incorporate them into the plan and local regulations. They must identify and describe with regulatory instruments opportunities that may not be relevant in the period concerned but must not be overlooked.

Another conflict is that the master development plan applies to the whole of the community, whereas the municipality directly may dispose of only its own property. Within the community many other entities have more maneuvering room than the municipality's own property. While previously the community was controlled in a uniform manner, whether locally or from the center, in line with the master development planning approach the situation now has become more complicated due to the evolving ownership structure, market conditions and democratic public administration.

What is the result of this? Municipal property management must serve the economy of the whole community. This is its fundamental function, and this is what local residents express their opinion on during local elections. The scale of the master development plan is dependent upon the community scale of municipal financial management. Municipal property management must think in terms of this scale as well.

The municipality as an economic entity has a fundamental interest in increasing its revenues and its assets in the long term. This interest is best expressed in the determination of value. In the interpretation represented here, the determination of value means market value. For purposes of municipal property policy the starting point must be the separation of property classes that are marketable, that have limited marketability and that are unmarketable. These classifications are used in the Municipal Act as well, but experience shows that municipalities do not adhere to them in their financial plans. In a market environment realistic local property and economic policy can be based only on the value of the property portfolio, the evaluation of its

ability to retain its value and an accurate estimate of its marketability.

The benefit of classification based on market value and marketability is that the separation of property elements with short- and long-term effects is possible; entrepreneurial property and elements affecting public services and their utilization can be incorporated in a uniform concept and implementation program that can be executed according to schedule.

It cannot be emphasized enough that, no matter which economic entity is concerned, in a market environment the key is to *think in terms of market value*; every element of financial management is a market factor. Such market factors include the labor and technology used, materials, energy and information.

Therefore, the valuation of municipal property and a value-centered financial approach must be extended to unmarketable property elements as well. If the revenue and expenditure structure of such property elements operates on financial and operational principles similar to those of marketable elements, merely increasing the budgetary revenue of a particular institution or infrastructural element from, say, fifteen to twenty percent is a significant positive development in itself. Savings can be interpreted as quasi-profits, because some of the funds previously spent on the entity concerned are freed. This, of course, presumes that the remaining, marketable part of the property increases its yield.

It is also natural, however, that the municipality will not use its property for business purposes according to pure market rules. A favorable approach is to finance municipal developments from the profits of property management or from self-generated revenues, not jeopardizing the funding of operating expenses.

If the market value of property elements is not determined, the economic potential and value of the total assets cannot be monitored in a market environment. Determination of the market value automatically identifies the local property elements and thus the financial position of the municipality. Otherwise the municipality would be unable to accurately identify the extent of replacement or value preservation required or the sector that may act as a driving force in the economy. *The problem of property depletion can be avoided.*

Thus, municipal property must be operated with a uniform economic approach, as a quasi-enterprise, with profitable and unprofitable property elements organizationally separated. Here the problem is that sociopolitical objectives must not be confused with economic profitability, because the quasi-entrepreneurial operation of municipal property may also be harmful. Today relationships are different between the municipality and its citizens, the municipality and a nonpublicly owned local economic entity. If the municipality runs its economic holdings as quasi-independent enterprises, it may view private enterprises with similar profiles as competitors in a particular scope of activity, and local entrepreneurs similarly may consider the market-type entities of the municipality as competitors. This may result in a number of conflicts and justified or unjustified accusations (personal interrelations, the monopolization of information, personal financial interests, illicit wealth accumulation, etc.). In previous election cycles directors of property management organizations ran for mayor and former mayors became heads of property management organizations. Another severe danger is that successful profit-oriented activities easily may lead to a confusion of roles (excessive emphasis on economic entrepreneurship), and the public role of the municipality to represent the interests of the whole community may be neglected.

1.7 CITY MARKETING

Community marketing has increased in significance in terms of attracting investors and cultivating good taxpayers and tourism. Its main subject is to "sell" (not sell out) the values of the community, presenting local demographic, cultural, educational and other features as well as taxation, administrative, housing and employment conditions. Effective community marketing must meet the following key requirements:

- vision and, to support this, a development strategy that encompasses the community's economic policy, communication with local residents, economic and civil organizations, interest groups and mechanisms of continuous interest conciliation;
- review and computerized processing of all types of information about the community, its benefits (values) and disadvantages;
- familiarity with potentially competing communities;
- identification, selection, prioritization and persuasion of "buyers," i.e., potential investors and consumers;
- compilation and prioritization of benefits, priority treatment of especially attractive relative advantages and their preparation for "sale";

- coordination of the work of various interest groups within the community in exploiting the values of the community on the market;
- coordination and cooperation with the microregion and the county.

The community marketing strategy must be directed within and without the community at the same time. The success of community marketing can be summarized in two expressions: credibility and local consciousness.

Credibility is important because the utilization of values and products of the community at realistic prices is a long-term interest. The living space of present and future generations is a very valuable asset, not a fashion item or clearance sale. It is also necessary that the investor feels confident and secure, is aware of advantages and disadvantages and senses the desire of locals to become partners.

Local consciousness is necessary because residents must have an attachment to their community not only on an emotional basis or through historic or cultural traditions, but also through knowledge of the economic and business potential of the settlement. The identity of citizens is related not only to birthplace but also to creative work and the formation of a social and economic environment. Excessive expectations are not useful, but neither is weak-hearted pessimism.

Citizens, economic organizations, NGOs and the municipality must think and behave along a generally accepted strategic program and plan in an identical manner. The message of community marketing must be reflected in the behavior of residents and organizations, as they are credible and permanent "advertising media." They judge what is superficial propaganda or fair business behavior. After all, community marketing is a communication activity, the primary purpose of which is to activate and connect external and internal resources and turn them into an economic message or offer.

The main breakthrough points of community development are improvement of transportation, communication, logistical and information infrastructures; the expansion of economic relations; the development of tourism; and the creation of a probusiness legal and economic environment. All this is related to the shaping of communication culture, market pervasion and thus marketing and public relations efforts. Consequently, community development strategy and community marketing activities must be developed hand in hand, naturally with the broad involvement of local opinion leaders, interest groups, NGOs and political organizations.

2 Local Government Capital Investments

The purpose of this section is to summarize the characteristics of local capital investments. The main questions are (1) how important are capital budgets at the local level and (2) how developed are property management and planning techniques. This section is heavily based on the information collected in the previous stages of this research project. Thus, the analysis of available fiscal data, case studies and the experiences of four countries in the Central and East European (CEE) region (see annex) provide the background for the statements made here.

The most important factor behind local capital investment policies is the *transfer of state-owned assets* to local governments, which became owners of enormous volumes of capital stock in a relatively short period of time that they were unprepared to use and manage. The value of local government assets was approximately HUF 1,000 billion. The composition of local assets was altered during the privatization process and the transfer of state-owned property to municipalities. In 1991 a majority of local assets was fixed (mostly real estate); later financial assets (shares) became equally important. By 1997 local real estate was allocated unequally among the major types of municipalities. Locally owned real estate was concentrated in villages with populations of one to five thousand (thirty-five percent) and was owned and managed directly by the municipalities. Large cities owned only eight percent of the negotiable part of local property; their assets were sold and their commercial entities (companies) manage the remainder.

The proportion of capital expenditure in local budgets has decreased slightly and exhibits annual fluctuations. In election years it is usually high (nineteen percent); during fiscal restriction periods it is low (in 1995, fourteen percent). Reconstruction occupies a very low position among capital expenditures; its current per capita value is only one-quarter of its size in 1993. The sectoral breakdown of local government capital expenditures has shifted from human public services to physical infrastructure—waste management, road construction, capital investments in the water sector and in other property management being most typical.

The level of capital expenditures is rather low in Hungary and the countries studied. A vast majority (ninety to ninety-five percent) of local budgets is spent on current expenditures. A lack of self-generated revenues makes capital investment projects dependent on national budget grants, which are earmarked and targeted transfers for centrally accepted capital improvement programs. There are several international technical assistance programs in these countries that have attempted to combine knowledge transfer with some capital investment or loan programs with limited success.

Forms of financing local government capital investments also are undeveloped. Loans are not used and municipal bonds are not issued, partly because local government financial management is not prepared for these techniques. A lack of incentives on the local government side increases distrust of private investors. Administrative procedures are not supportive and have high indirect costs.

Two-thirds of local government capital revenues are from asset sales. A majority of the capital sold was fixed, but now the sale of financial assets (shares) is most typical (forty-four percent of revenues from asset sales). These one-time revenues are major sources for capital expenditures, so as they slowly diminish, the level of investment also decreases.

Total capital revenue is already three-fourths of capital expenditure (plus revenues from municipal borrowing). As the composition of local property shifts from negotiable commercial property to core property that cannot be sold, local governments are less able to finance their capital investments from the one-time sale of assets. Capital revenues are highly concentrated: forty-four percent of all revenue is raised in Budapest. In the countryside capital revenues are generally proportionate to total local revenues; only towns and cities with populations of ten to twenty thousand are able to collect higher capital revenues. Transfers within the public sector are most significant in small municipalities (with populations of two to five thousand) and in county local governments. Capital revenues from external sources are most typical in municipalities with populations of two to ten thousand, as the users of utilities typically contribute to investments directly. In large cities these revenues are less significant.

Interestingly, not only the size of local government influences the composition of capital revenues. For example, in the northern trans-Danubian region capital revenues from transfers within the public sector and revenues raised outside the public sector are relatively high. The schemes of capital investments here probably attract more external revenues.

The case studies revealed that years after the political turnover and the major privatization waves, local governments still do not have a concise overview of real estate-marked dynamics in their municipalities. However, it generally is accepted that real estate values represent real demand. This is more obvious in municipalities where there is high demand (e.g., in Balatonboglár or Veresegyház) or where there is a longer market tradition (as in Kecskemét or Eger). Demand price determinants include location, clear ownership structures, utility services and accessibility.

The analysis of price fluctuations identified the main market trends. As most municipalities do not monitor real estate prices and the information derived from published sources and local agents is only indicative, the exercise was not fully successful; thus, this relationship is not demonstrated here. One of the lessons gleaned from the case studies is even more important for local governments. The municipality should monitor the market closely, as real estate values can be interpreted as aggregate indicators for environmental quality, economic environment, infrastructural capacity and local potential, problems and opportunities. In larger cities information is available at property management offices, while in smaller settlements the mayor usually can provide a good overview. Unfortunately, such knowledge does not influence most decisions made by the local government.

Capital investments are influenced by urban plans. After the transition general urban development plans were outdated and new plans were drafted. In some cases general plans were preceded by site layout schemes and detailed regulatory plans to be incorporated into the general development plan later, as developments occurred at a speed that did not allow the necessary time to elaborate such large-scale plans. In the case of smaller settlements general plans were not used much even before the transition, as the relative simplicity of the local situation allowed direct decision making.

The most important aim of the newly prepared general development plans is to provide space for extensive urban development by incorporating land on the peripheries of developed areas. It is well known that new enterprises, especially large ones, prefer green field investment, as land is cheaper, there are less restrictions concerning conformity with the surrounding developed environment, the investor-developer has better chances to negotiate favorable terms with the authorities, and there are no demolition costs or unexpected contamination issues.

It is also common that no urban development concept and program precedes the regulatory planning process. Development strategies are formulated only during the final stage of physical plan making. As a result, this has little influence on the adopted regulatory plan, which is modified later in accordance with changing development strategies.

Development concepts remain strictly in the physical and technical realm. Based on the case studies, it is not recommended that physical planning professionals take a *dominant role* in the preparation of the development concept. The emphasis that should be given to these aspects over other development issues (like local economy, the creation of workplaces, etc.) is a strategic question.

3 Financing Municipal Capital Investments

Local capital investment and development policies now are influenced by two major factors: (1) highly restrictive fiscal environment and (2) increasing involvement of the private sector in financing capital investments. Economic decline in the early 1990s resulted in the slow erosion of national sources for capital expenditures. High inflation decreased the real value of national grants. Self-generated revenues could not compensate these losses, and available resources mostly financed the current budget; operation and management were the primary goals of local fiscal policy.

The trend to cut back capital expenditures during a period of fiscal austerity is typical in every country. The usual ratio of a one-percent increase in infrastructure together with a one-percent increase in GNP cannot be maintained; capital expenditures are decreased or postponed. This was the case in the 1980s in many developing countries that implemented adjustment programs and in Great Britain where the budget deficit was high [Chandavarkar 1994].

Concurrent with decreasing public funds, the private sector has become more involved in financing infrastructure capital investments. Local governments operate in a market environment and have to cooperate with private

actors in many ways. The relationship between municipalities and local businesses is most visible in local property-related actions and economic development. Components of local government activities influence the local economy through financing and the management of services. Local administration as a public authority is a key factor as well.

Table 6 indicates the four main types of relationship between local governments and the private sector. Traditional business development through sharing information and providing advice has direct impact on the local entrepreneurial climate. Property management is a key component of such relationships. It is often emphasized in this study that local businesses are affected by the other two local activities as well.

One major area of mutual interest is the provision of public services. Local governments as clients rely on the private sector when services are contracted out. Alternative service delivery arrangements and public-private partnerships often are based on cofinancing schemes. The parties to such cooperation are not necessarily businesses, but the business climate is influenced by local values in service provision. Municipalities also influence the local economy through taxation and other administrative functions.

Table 6
Relationship between Local Governments and Businesses

Local Government	Entrepreneur
1. *Actor in Local Economic Development:* Business Advice Information Sharing	Employer Voter
2. *Owner of Property* [buildings, plots]: Investment Partner Supplier of Renting Units	Investor Renter
3. *Service Provider:* Client Financing Capital Investments	Contractor, service producer Partner in cofinancing
4. *Local authority:* Taxing Power Licensing	Taxpayer Applicant, partner

The second column in table 6 shows the various faces of business. All are equally important for local government economic development activities. As unemployment is a major local problem, businesses have a primary role in providing jobs. Entrepreneurs and managers also create a strong community, so as voters or lobbying groups they are important partners to local governments. In public service delivery and capital investment local governments have to communicate with the private sector. Financial contacts exist through taxation and real estate development.

In this section, three elements of public-private relationship will be discussed. The primary focus is on property-related contacts between local governments and the private sector. First, the role of property management in local economic development; second, municipalities as owners of real estate; and finally, municipalities as service providers will be detailed. Local taxation as a fiscal tool will be presented with other mechanisms for linking property and the local budget.

3.1 PROPERTY MANAGEMENT AND LOCAL ECONOMIC DEVELOPMENT

Local governments face various problems due to the evolving economic environment. Economic stagnation, restructuring of traditional sectors, unemployment, lack of capital and underdeveloped financial services forced them to launch local remedies. In the first period of the new local government system there were high expectations for raising revenues from municipal economic activities. However the "entrepreneurial local government" was an illusion; direct involvement of public entities in business activities was unsuccessful for two reasons. First, local governments were not winners in the privatization process. Second, they could not manage entrepreneurial and investor roles properly. Local councils were not able to act efficiently as owners; leading officials and politicians did not have the authority of "managers." Local government administration had no experience in dealing with fiscal management problems and did not have the organizational capability to operate in a business environment.

Despite these failures local governments have developed various indirect methods of economic development. According to the survey presented in this study, in 1994 there were four major local goals: (1) to promote inward investment, (2) to provide new jobs, (3) to support the restructuring of agriculture and (4) to develop the service

sector [Péteri 1994]. Preferences varied by type of local government. In Budapest and in cities the service sector and inward investments were primary goals. In villages, which were hit hardest by unemployment, job creation and the development of agriculture through investment were preferred.

Local governments adopted two types of strategies for business promotion. On one hand, they searched for large investors that would provide a significant number of job opportunities, buy available land and have a multiplying effect on the local economy through new business activities. On the other hand, local political statements mostly targeted small and medium-sizes enterprises (SMEs), which were important to the service sector and provided a favorable business climate for large investors. Sometimes SME development was supported to win votes from a social group that had a strong voice in the community.

Property-related activities are crucial—but not the most important—methods of local economic development. Public utility infrastructure and direct contacts with investors are preferred for attracting new investment capital and for decreasing unemployment. Listing available property typically supports local economic development in these areas; local governments use subsidized sale or free transfer of plots and real estate less frequently. However, subsidized rent and the allocation of plots are preferred techniques for supporting small businesses [see Péteri 1994].

Local governments attract new businesses through various methods of promotion and city marketing. One technique is to publish information booklets on the municipality's economic conditions and investment opportunities. General information often is supplemented by more specific data on industrial premises available in the area. This property-related information includes real estate units owned by both the local government and private companies.

In a mail survey, economic information brochures and promotional materials of city and county local governments were collected, primarily on investment opportunities and real estate offers. Correspondence indicated that best practices were solicited. Perhaps this fact explained the low response rate: approximately one-fifth of local governments replied. The following brief evaluation is based on this sample.[9]

Seven of the nineteen county local governments responded. Interestingly all are in regions hit by economic decline.

63

However, the quality of these information booklets is quite good. Some were produced in cooperation with the local enterprise development agency and supported by Phare or other technical assistance programs. This reflects the new character of county local government: a coordinating role with indirect influence on municipal local governments.

Information brochures typically introduce the general economic and social conditions of the county. The length of such studies varies, but they clearly show that local governments understand the importance of human, environmental and recreational conditions to investors. Information on real estate is detailed; property data are sometimes combined with an introduction to the leading companies in the region. Information on available real estate units includes the most important characteristics of plots and buildings: size, location, facilities, zoning, etc. Typically they are produced in English, and in three cases, in German. One county produced a compact disc version of economic and real estate information (Szabolcs-Szatmar county, one of the poorest regions but an experimental area for regional development projects under the Phare program).

Large cities follow a different strategy for business promotion. In the sample of ten cities only four have detailed lists of available property units (one on floppy disc). The rest place emphasis on general information about the city, introducing local government policies towards inward investments; for example, local tax policy, user charges and budget information often are included. Cities with county rights already have established internal units for business promotion; thus, general information on the city is focused on the company, department or nonprofit agency that actually negotiates with potential investors, supporting individual treatment of the partner. These companies or units can develop better deals, as they influence local government policies and the major utility companies in the city (Tatabánya).

Medium-sized cities and small towns typically provide general information for investors and potential partners. They often focus on tourism and recreational attractions. Only a few have detailed property information, and almost none present the neighboring villages or the subregion. This fact demonstrates that these cities have only a limited number of attractive real estate units. They understand that investors prefer large cities, so they can compete only if other investment conditions are developed.

The survey indicates that local governments have devised their own strategies concerning real estate development and business promotion. The county local governments play only an indirect role in the Hungarian legal system, but in economically depressed regions they are very active. Large cities do attract investors, as they have available real estate and organizational units for managing the negotiation process. Small cities and towns have only limited offers, so their city marketing is focused on recreational and environmental areas.

3.2   LOCAL GOVERNMENT PROPERTY

Property-related municipal economic development activities are determined by regulations on property transfer and ownership rights. Legislation on local governments and the transfer of state-owned property created two major types of local assets: core property and negotiable, transferable assets. Core municipal property has two categories: nontransferable and assets with limited capacity to sell.

Core, nontransferable property includes local roads and public spaces. Core assets with restricted rights are utilities, public buildings, protected historic sites and any other local assets dedicated to this group of property. Sale of these assets requires council decision. For protected and historic buildings the agreement of the relevant ministry also is needed. Any other utilization of core property (e.g. concession, renting) is based on local decision.

In 1997 the 820 thousand real estate units of local governments had a book value of HUF 853 billion, but only one-fifth of this stock was assessed or had a value higher than zero. Most real estate units are negotiable (forty-seven percent), but a considerably large part is core property, which cannot be sold (forty-one percent). The rest (eleven percent) can be negotiated only under certain conditions with the approval of the council. Property with limited negotiability represents fifty-two percent of the total book value of local real estate.

3.2.1 Property Management Regulations and Practices

Basic laws drove property transfer and local management practices. Similar to other aspects of transition, there was a strong belief in the influence and effectiveness of legal regulation. Acts on local government and on municipal property transfer together with the compulsory transformation of state-owned companies created a regulatory environment in which economic and financial incentives were hidden in legal texts. Contrary to the legal approach there was a considerable negotiating element involved in property transfer. The unique task of demolishing former unified state-owned property cannot be resolved only by legal action. Based on general rules property transfer committees were established in each county to discuss and manage all technical details. This gave local governments some flexibility.

The legal approach did not work for all aspects of property transfer. Later scandals in the privatization of state-owned companies (when municipal shares from undeveloped areas were not allocated from the property agency to the new owners) showed that there was room for political maneuvering. The privatization of gas utilities was a case in the Constitutional Court in which local governments were successful in defending their assets.

Rather strict local property transfer legislation was favorable to local governments, and the political trend towards decentralization in the early 1990s supported the transfer of assets. However, local governments were unprepared to manage the unexpectedly large volume of local property efficiently. Understanding the importance of their new assets, local governments intended to control most property-related decisions. Locally established rules usually placed councils in a position to control almost every step of property management.

In such a legal and organizational environment business motivation and interest should come through political mechanisms. High pressure from domestic and international investors for land and other real estate units led to asset sales of significant volumes. Local governments, lacking other major self-generated revenues, sold their fixed assets. According to the reports of the State Audit Office local councils did not control the negotiable component of local property, and the sale of municipal assets was not always managed in a competitive process [ÁSZ 1994]. Local governments thus found themselves in an "either-or" position: either they maintained direct control over local property, or their assets were sold to the private sector. In the first case, public sector values and political decision-making procedures influenced property management, and in the second case, municipalities practically lost control over assets and property development.

There were two basic regulations that were intended to improve local government property management and protect municipal assets. Former social apartments were sold extensively. Local government kept only six percent of the total housing stock (235 thousand units); the rest was sold mostly to residents. The law on municipal property transfer forced local governments to put all such revenues into a local housing fund, which could be used only for residential building. Due to restrictive fiscal conditions that forced a low return for such apartments, these funds were not sufficient for the construction of significant local housing. Any other uses of the housing fund (e.g., subsidies, social grants) were regarded as semi-legal actions. Therefore, this regulation did not protect local assets successfully.[10]

A second regulation also supported decentralized actions by establishing a unified system of *property registration*. This primarily served central information needs but had an indirect effect on local behavior. In order to provide data for the compulsory national registry, local governments had to create proper inventories of their own property. Unfortunately the national property register focused on the physical characteristics of assets, but it served as the initial basis for valuation and assessment of municipal property, helping to clarify the legal status of property units and determine the utilization of assets. In this manner, local government physical assets were not integrated into the fiscal system, as current revenues (or revenue potential) on property management were not incorporated into local budgets.

During the first years of the new local government system property management was a major problem. Local politicians and officials recognized the potential value of the new local assets, but property management techniques were undeveloped. The primary reason for inefficient management was confusion concerning property management goals. Local governments owned buildings and plots for public services that were used very extensively, but they were not able to develop efficient property management techniques for this group of assets "with limited negotiability." Actual maintenance costs were not compared to the potential revenue of alternative uses. Thus, these public property units typically were regarded as being without any value.

The second group of real estate units was for business purposes. Here local economic development goals were clearly recognized. Sale, rent and joint investment opportunities were available and used frequently. No other more direct involvement of real estate development techniques were used. Even the professional term "property management" did not reflect the active character of "real estate development."

65

Here, it is assumed that local government asset management is connected to local economic development in two ways: (1) through utilization of real estate and (2) through management and development of physical infrastructure. Only the first is discussed here; the infrastructure development aspects are presented in the following chapter: how local governments through their ownership and service delivery rights are able to influence local business activities. There is also an indirect effect of these local actions, which is important for entrepreneurs and investors: how economic development is built into local decision making. This "soft" aspect of local government actions includes everything from building access roads to developing new business areas through municipal investments in human services and business-friendly local administration.

There are three major *stages of property management.* In the preparatory stage, ownership information and registration are developed; for economic analysis, property-running costs are identified. Active implementation involves analysis of rented municipal property units and regular review of buildings, plots and other real estate. The third evaluation stage includes control and assessment of local property management [Audit Commission 1988; Péteri 1995].

Local governments in Hungary use some elements of these management techniques. Present practices face two major problems. First, management methods rarely establish a closed system. Registry and decision-making competencies are usually set, but there are no independent organizations to implement municipal policies or regular property reviews. Second, there often is no direct relationship between property management and local fiscal decisions, because municipal assets in real estate are not evaluated. Assessment of available property should be compared to running and amortization costs. These costs depend on the methods and efficiency of property utilization. Local government property management policy should be incorporated into the municipal service delivery strategy as one cost factor.

Real estate development techniques are different from public property management methods. Developers connect future users of the real estate with capital markets and investors. Local governments might participate in the development process as owners of real estate units and as local public bodies (regulators, politicians). In the public sector real estate development requires professional and personal abilities. Many actors of different characters and with various motives are involved. The decision-making process also is more complicated, as private and public goals must match.

Perhaps the most visible examples of urban real estate development recently are shopping malls. In large cities these retail trade and amusement facilities became dominant factors of urban life by the second half of the 1990s. In Budapest and its urban area seventeen large malls were opened. Their gross area is more than 450 thousand square meters, and the cost of capital investment varies between HUF 2 and 10 billion [*Magyar Hírlap* 1998]. An additional 350 thousand square meters of units are planned for the urban area of Budapest [Lukovich 1997]. These new units will modify significantly the structure of traditional retail trade units; it is estimated that the current forty percent turnover in malls will increase to seventy percent.

Shopping malls and new office buildings have an impact not only on urban life but also on property value. Local governments are able to make one-time revenue from selling land, but they also are faced with the consequences of these capital investments. Positive outcomes include the multiplying effect on local businesses, increase in neighboring property value, etc. Negative effects may be significant as well: increased congestion, rising transportation costs and the transformation of the urban environment. This example shows that there are winners and losers in large-scale property development. Local governments as public bodies have the responsibility to balance development gains and losses.

In the process of making property management decisions local governments have to balance costs and benefits, which are measured not only in economic but also in social terms. Thus, planning and preparation are very important to property management decisions. Legal, physical and financial feasibility should be tested and compared to government goals. To meet public requirements real estate developers are faced with some specific characteristics of public property-related decisions [ICMA 1989].

Local governments prefer to control their property units directly. Very often they do not sell their real estate, even if the market price is favorable, because they hope to maintain public trust. Another characteristic of public bodies is risk avoidance, which is preferred to making losses on property through sales or utilization at some level of risk. Local governments often operate in a restrictive fiscal environment in which their short-term objective is to use capital revenues for current expenditures. This explains some irrational economic behavior in real estate development. There are also motivations other than profit for local governments in their property management activities (jobs, environmental protection, etc.)

Real estate management techniques of local governments are grouped into two categories. The first is direct involvement in property management by selling or leasing buildings and land. Local governments can follow other development strategies to obtain higher revenues or other benefits: renewal or construction increases rent and value, participation of developers in investment provides additional capital, the exchange of sites serves the urban planning strategy of the city, etc. The second option is direct municipal involvement in local businesses with local government property. Local governments are allowed to take only limited risks, so their economic development objectives should be reached in this special legal and decision-making environment. The most typical forms of local economic development with municipal property are industrial (business) parks and incubator units, managed workplaces. Both are intended to attract inward investments and to support start-up businesses. Industrial parks and incubators are well-served investment areas or rented units under special conditions.

Local governments also invest in businesses, typically through their management companies or subsidiaries. Local development companies support many start-up businesses for limited periods of time in the crisis regions of Great Britain, and local property can serve as a mortgage guarantee for a local enterprise.

These techniques of deeper municipal involvement in local economic development should be separate from political decision making. This can be attained only if decision-making procedures and the organizational setting do not support direct political influence. Local real estate development companies, as separate commercial entities under indirect local control, should assume these tasks.

3.3 LOCAL INFRASTRUCTURAL DEVELOPMENT

The third dimension of relationships between local governments and the private sector is the provision of public services, including infrastructural development. Municipalities have primary responsibility for various fundamental physical services and have indirect influence on almost all other elements of the infrastructure. Thus, the local government as a *service provider* can influence the local business climate. Urban productivity can be increased through the concentration of production factors by achieving economies of scale and agglomeration economies: economies of scale in capital-intensive services result in decreasing unit costs proportionate to the size of the infrastructure; agglomeration economies involve the combination of economic activities supporting more efficient use of production factors.

Infrastructure is an important asset of local government not only as equity but also as stable *revenue-producing property*. The municipal infrastructure is comprised of mostly core, nonnegotiable assets. The market value of these assets usually is above their registered (book) value. Infrastructure is important for local budgets, as it enables municipalities to define future revenues stemming from the utilization of these assets. Transformation of the structure of assets on the local government balance sheet reflects changes in municipal property. Real estate was the primary fixed asset for local governments before the extensive "municipalization" of infrastructure and privatization of state-owned enterprises were initiated. Five years later, when most of the housing stock had been sold, public service companies were established, and the forms of local ownership were restructured. Almost one-third of local government assets were financial (shares and dividends).

Table 7
Local Government Real Estate and Financial Assets

Year	Real Estate [% of total assets]	Shares, Dividends [% of total assets]
1991	57.8	1.5
1992	41.6	28.3
1993	37.5	29.1
1994	35.3	30.9
1995	35.8	29.7

Local governments became owners of four thousand commercial entities with a combined value of HUF 355 billion. Mostly these companies provided mandatory public services, so they were established as components of the infrastructure. These assets are highly concentrated in Budapest and in other cities; thus, they primarily benefit urban municipalities, influence local economic development and can produce significant revenues.

Table 8
Locally Owned Enterprises [1994]

	Counties	Budapest	Cities	Villages	Total
Locally Owned Enterprises					
Number	146	553	2,103	1,272	4,074
%	3.6	13.6	51.6	31.2	100.0
Shares [HUF billions]	5.2	259.7	86.2	4.0	355.1
%	1.5	73.1	24.3	1.1	100.0
Enterprises for Mandatory Services					
Number	18	30	260	400	708
%	2.6	4.2	36.7	56.5	100.0
Shares [HUF billions]	0.5	236.3	52.9	1.8	291.5
%	0.2	81.1	18.1	0.6	100.0
Population [%]	—	*18.1*	*44.6*	*37.3*	*100.0*
Expenditures [%]	*19.9*	*26.2*	*36.9*	*17.0*	*100.0*
Shares in Mandatory Service Enterprises					
% of total shares	9.0	91.0	61.3	45.0	82.1

Figure 1
Service Delivery Arrangements

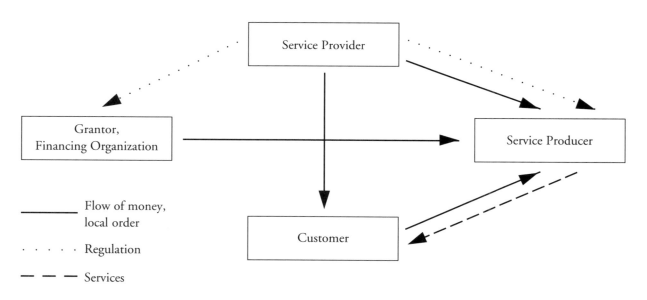

Local governments and businesses are connected in two ways: in operation and management of services as clients and contractors, and in financing capital investments as partners. In *service delivery* the client-contractor split is the basis for utilization of local government assets. Local governments are able to pay for services produced by the private sector. Alternatively the municipality as a regulatory authority is able to create revenue flow from customers to the private service unit. Under these service delivery arrangements there are four basic actors: service provider, producer, customer and the financing organization.

There are three main types of service delivery arrangements under this general scheme: contracting out, franchise and concession (a fourth form of service management, which is primarily focused on capital investments, will be discussed later). Obviously the three service delivery techniques have various forms in practice and sometimes are combined.

Under *contracting out* arrangements the local government as a client enters a contractual agreement with the private entity to provide the service for a group of consumers. These services are purchased from the contractor and are paid directly by the government or by the customer. In the latter case the price usually is controlled by government decisions. Public bodies are obligated to monitor and control service delivery. There are various forms of contracting out, as the timeframe of the contract varies, methods of payments change and risks and assets are shared between the client (service provider) and the company (service producer).

Most typically contracting out is used for operational and maintenance work, so contracts cover relatively short periods. The length of contracts should be long enough to finance the capital used during that period. Depending on the type of assets required for the service, the contract period may be different: in capital intensive sectors, like solid waste collection, it usually is five to seven years, and cleaning of office space is often only one year.

User charges (prices) are crucial elements of contracts, especially for public services for which costs are not accounted properly. There are two main types of contracts: fixed price and cost. In the latter the local government takes the risk of cost increases. It is extremely important to agree on price adjustment indices in CEE economies, where the rate of inflation is high. Otherwise private contractors will not invest within the contract period, and the potential efficiency gains will not be reached.

There are various schemes that aim to distribute risk between the client and the contractor. The agreed price mechanism, ownership of fixed assets and replacement costs of various elements of capital are all topics of negotiation. Most typically local governments keep ownership of basic assets (e.g., the landfill), and contractors provide equipment or other small capital investments (e.g., compactor at the landfill).

If the local government wants to maintain direct control over the service producing company, a *management contract* is signed. In this case the management of the public enterprise shares the risk of running the company with the municipality. Contracts for public service delivery with exclusive rights to provide the service are called *concessions*. They often are combined with the implementation of capital investment. Law restricts services that can be operated through concession agreements. Concession agreements also define the legal form of operation, so the contractor (lessee) is responsible for capital assets financed by the concession. This separation of assets helps to measure capital and current costs in order to identify financing sources. The government transfers the right to set and collect user charges or tariffs paid for the service. As concession agreements cover very long periods (in Hungary, a maximum of thirty-five years), clear regulations on service performance and agreements on contract termination are necessary. If the producer sets and collects charges, concession agreements are called *franchises*. Under franchise agreements, the local government does not control the price of the service, but also it does not guarantee a monopolistic position for the service producer (e.g., restaurants, funeral services).

These classical models of alternative service delivery arrangements do not always work properly in Hungary. There are several problems with local government management approaches and techniques that hinder efficiency gains from these innovations. Based on the case studies and other examples, local governments are not able to utilize their service delivery rights as municipal assets for the following reasons.

1. *Owner and client roles are not separated.* It is often more important for the local government as majority owner of the service organization to protect the interest of the company than to keep service standards high. When the service producer has a strong influence on municipal

decisions the local government typically is not able to control cost increases, safety of the service is given great emphasis in contracts, and the primary goal of the municipality is to keep its assets in their present form. In this situation the need for an increased level of service performance, lower labor costs and leaner service organization cannot be enforced. The local government as owner of the service organization controls the function of maintaining a high level of service.

2. *Lack of service performance indicators or monitoring.* When the client's role is not properly defined, the local government does not have the technical capacity to develop a service strategy. Without a strategy there are no service specifications, which thus are not translated into standards and performance indicators. When outputs are not measurable, crucial components of service contracts are missing. In this situation the local government is not able to control the contractor, and the lack of monitoring might lead to poor services or bankruptcy of the service organization. In these cases the municipality as the ultimate service provider should accept the burden of corrections and cost increases.

3. *Lack of negotiating capacity.* Contracting with the private sector requires competent negotiating parties on the local government side. Both politicians and staff should have clear goals, transparent procedures and effective service control measures in negotiating with the private sector. Very often these conditions do not exist simultaneously. Typically, elected officials promote contracting out for efficiency gains, but without a clear service strategy the staff is unprepared for process management. In other cases the local administration supports contracts with the private sector, but local politicians express reluctance; lacking transparent selection procedures, they fear accusations of corruption.

4. *Loss of control over service prices.* Public utility services primarily are financed by user charges; at the very least operational costs are covered by the price of the service. Local government is the price-setting authority in all major services: water, sewage, solid waste collection, district heating, rent. No subsidies exist with the exception of water tariffs. Typically these user charges are not accounted in the local government budget, as the service organization has the right to collect these public revenues directly. Thus, the local government as owner of the service organization with price-setting authority is not capable of counterbalancing the pressure of the company for price increases. Financial information on actual and planned service costs also comes from the service organization, which makes local justification even harder. Agreements on formulas for price increases (input-based or maximized rate of return) often are not built into the service contracts.

5. *Lack of competition.* Legislation on compulsory urban services requires tendering under Hungarian law (e.g., in the case of solid waste collection). Modern public procurement regulations specify tendering procedures. Despite these clear sets of legislation, current practice is different: municipalities argue their ownership right to define the form of service delivery and refer to continuation of previous contractual agreements with the same companies. Lacking regular control on service effectiveness and cost efficiency without tendering, local governments are not able to place benchmarks on their service organizations.

Local governments typically cooperate with the private sector in service areas that require high capital investments. Public utilities and communal services are capital intensive, so the *lack of municipal capital* revenues was mostly behind alternative service arrangements. Both in operation and development there is a high need for *technology transfer*, which is another factor for promoting contracting out and concessions.

In *build-operate-transfer (BOT) schemes* private capital is involved in financing government projects. Private investors finance construction, and the government pays back the capital and interest by contracting the private company. Sources of financing projects are charges and other payments made by the users of the utilities. Thus, lenders and investors in these projects mostly depend on cash flow generated by the investment. Transfer of the right to operate the infrastructure keeps ownership rights with the public body. When the project costs are covered (depending on the type of project, usually twenty to twenty-five years), the government takes over the assets and the right to run the service.

Typically, BOT schemes are used for those physical infrastructural services that generate revenues through user charges. There are many sectors that are financed through BOT schemes: the energy sector (power plant, refineries), transportation (toll roads) and waste management (water and wastewater plants, landfills). Capital investment projects using BOT schemes involve three main actors: the owner (government), the project company and the investors or lenders (banks). Technical details of BOT schemes will be discussed later.

Local infrastructure development is financed through several sources, and the combinations of these revenues create various models. BOT schemes are only one group of financing techniques; other revenue sources dominate local capital investments in Hungary. The following section will outline the major types and mechanisms of capital project financing.

3.3.1 Financing Models

Infrastructure financing techniques have to cope with the economic and technical characteristics of public utilities and urban services. First, infrastructure services have extended distribution networks and large operating equipment; therefore, capital investment costs are high, requiring accumulation of capital before the project is initiated. Competitiveness is reduced due to the costly and timely process of entering and leaving the sector. Together with long pay-off periods, these factors lead to longer debt maturities and high debt-equity ratios [Chandavarkar 1994]. Local capital investments in infrastructure require diverse sources of funding: national grants, revenues from local budgets, contributions paid by future users and private capital in the forms of loans and other financing arrangements. Only with a combination of these sources can the goals of infrastructure development be met.

Grants from higher levels of government are needed to finance capital projects with significant external effects. Utilities have a positive effect on the environment, which is the primary concern of national policy. The wider community indirectly benefits from local infrastructure development, so only the host (gestor) municipality cannot finance it. Projects usually extend beyond municipal borders; otherwise economies of scale cannot be achieved. These spillovers should be funded through joint financing schemes or by higher levels of government.

For efficient decision making on public infrastructure capital investments, the financial burden and benefits received should be matched. A matching ratio expresses how the wider community contributes to the capital investment, which is different by sectors and groups of municipalities involved in a project. It expresses national preferences (e.g., sewage is more important than solid waste treatment) and incentives (in the case of cooperation among municipalities, the matching ratio is ten percent higher). Under current Hungarian legislation all local governments applying for matching grants are eligible for funding (assuming that they meet the technical and administrative criteria). The purpose of this law was the nondiscretionary allocation of matching grants.

In the early 1990s the outcome of this rule was an excessive burden on the national budget, resulting in protectionist methods: (1) total costs of capital projects were capped and (2) local applications for matching grants were transferred to subsequent fiscal years. The consequence of the first technique was an increase in capital project costs of local governments, as they aspire to receive the maximum level of grants. The matching grant ratio with a cap on total costs resulted in a grant per unit of the infrastructure project (e.g., HUF per cubic meter). These grants were differentiated only by the size of the project; no other cost factors were taken into consideration, which gave local governments unequal handicaps, as their initial conditions were different (by geography, urban character, etc.). Setting priorities among local government capital grant applications also overpoliticized the process. Later this legislation was modified and feasibility studies were required as primary conditions for awarding grants. Mandatory coordination among various national funds also was introduced to avoid high ratios of nonlocal sources of infrastructure financing.

This latter regulation was a reaction to the extrabudgetary funds that allocated grants for capital investments in various sectors; local governments had access to national grants from the water, environmental and road funds. The sectoral ministries controlled these off-budget funds, and there was no coordination among various national sources. This led to high and unplanned matching ratios in local capital projects, reaching sixty to seventy percent of total capital costs. The national fiscal policymakers were also against these extrabudgetary funds as the Ministry of Finance did not control their operation. The latest fiscal legislation launched changes in both areas: coordination is compulsory and off-budget funds are part of the respective ministry chapters, which are more controlled.

International experience shows that there are various forms of development intermediaries that may finance municipal capital investments [Davey 1988]. Most try to combine banking operations with grants. Revolving funds produce accumulated capital for financing local projects by claiming repayment under favorable conditions. Some funds and development banks combine technical assistance and training with loans. Usually these funds supplement national grant schemes, as they influence the technical character of local capital projects.

Serious arguments are made against these intermediaries, usually by fiscal policymakers. Development funds are not as disciplined as other units of the general government budget. As stable revenue flows are appropriated to these funds (e.g., environmental fines, petrol tax) increasing proportions of government revenues escape direct control. Those funds that provide subsidized loans cannot work as financial institutions, so high arrears accumulate due to the low repayment culture of municipalities. Often these financial intermediaries are not funded sufficiently, decreasing their significance to local governments.

In Hungary the number of extrabudgetary funds decreased severely during the waves of fiscal restriction in 1995 and in 1998. Now most operate as special appropriations in the relevant ministry's budget, so the funds lost their quasi-independence and program-oriented character. The argument that they are separate "pockets of money" of the sectoral ministries is valid, as transparency and opportunities for joint decision making by several government organs have declined.

Available matching grants and transfers from extrabudgetary funds have an impact on local government development behavior. They usually operate in a grant-giving local fiscal environment, so a grant-seeking attitude dominates their capital investments. In cooperation with service companies they are motivated to propose large projects with the aim of acquiring large grants. Very often capital grant schemes encourage local investments, but no form of evaluation exists to determine service efficiency [Jokay et al. 1998].

Self-generated local government revenues such as *user charges* and *taxes* are critical elements for financing infrastructural development. In principle these revenues provide the balance between benefits received from improved infrastructure and the costs of capital investment. In practice user charges reflect demand and cover mostly operational and maintenance costs. Depreciation is usually a component of the user charge formula, but funds for new capital investments rarely are built into the price of municipal infrastructure.

As local taxes produce insignificant municipal revenues, none of the classical techniques for infrastructure financing can be used. In countries with developed property taxation systems, special assessments and betterment levies are earmarked revenues for capital investment financing. The benefit principle can be realized if increased tax revenues can be connected to future capital projects.

The financing of large-scale infrastructure projects requires cooperation among several autonomous local governments. In order to finance capital investments jointly, beneficiaries establish associations or other forms of cooperation. Under Hungarian legislation these joint units have no authority to define taxes or user charges for their autonomous member municipalities. As there are no elected bodies at the association level, tax- or price-setting authority cannot be delegated to that level of government. The lack of legal and management structures of special districts is one of the main constraints on the establishment of intermunicipal organizations of efficient and rational size.

There are arguments against betterment levies and special districts as the main sources of infrastructure finance. First, earmarking of local government financing threatens the unity of local budgets. This often-cited statement is used mostly by financial managers both at the local and national levels. However, local politicians and service managers prefer clear combinations of infrastructure projects and finances. The real danger is when the sectoral breakdown of local budgets is too rigid and, instead of program-oriented planning and financing, leads to overinvestment in some service areas. Without control over sectoral spending and lacking "sunset" legislation, fragmented revenues and expenditures might endanger the balance of local budgets.

In addition to tariffs and local taxes there is another group of financial contributions. *Users of the future infrastructure pay hook-up fees and infrastructure development fees.* Very often these sources of capital investment are not represented in the fiscal information system, but they are significant sources for capital projects. In the water sector most rural networks were built with the assistance of community water associations, which were then utilized as the organizational frameworks for the collection of private financial contributions. Subsidized loans are available through these associations, and participation can be compulsory if a majority of households concur with these schemes.

Private contributions for development projects are not reflected in local budgets, but local governments have an active role in creating and informally supporting these community associations. The relatively low level of local taxation usually is explained by the significant private contribution to infrastructure capital projects. Thus, fees for telephone service, natural gas and water are integrated into the local revenue policy.

Public-private partnership

The fourth component of infrastructure financing sources is private capital. Despite the grant-seeking character of local governments, municipal capital investments are dependent on the private sector. In general infrastructure projects are financed primarily by new equity or debt and less by retained earnings. The traditional argument for public involvement in projects with long repayment periods has been modified slightly. Governments establish partnerships with the private sector, and the excess capital available on the market is in constant search of stable and long-term investment options.

Local governments in Hungary are dependent on private sector involvement in capital investment for several reasons. First, significant pressure to improve performance and service standards requires *technology transfer* to the capital-intensive infrastructure. As modern technology can be used efficiently if professional and management practices also are developed, the transfer is combined with some form of direct involvement of ownership or financing schemes.

Local government capital projects are dependent on national grants, but substantial funding is needed to initiate application procedures. Municipalities cooperate with design and construction companies to finance the *start-up costs* of infrastructure projects [see Jokay et al. 1998]. Private companies usually finance the initial design and preparatory work of capital projects with hopes of getting contracts when the grant is awarded. There are semi-legal schemes of transferring advances to local budgets as well, which cover the "self-generated" portion of the future capital investment project. Municipalities often are faced with *liquidity problems*, as grants can be withdrawn only in predefined installments. Implementation can be accelerated with private sector involvement, which assists the more rapid flow of revenue.

Not only local government needs but also pressure from the private sector fuels partnership arrangements. Acting as a price-setting authority, local government is able to create a *stable revenue* base. Municipal real estate and balanced local budgets can serve as *collateral* for borrowing by the private sector. With local government guarantees, utility companies can borrow more easily. Sometimes municipal bonds are bought by the private sector and paid back from the future operating revenues collected by utility companies.

All these conditions for public and private partnerships in financing local infrastructure prove that service delivery rights are significant municipal assets. The necessary condition for efficient utilization of these assets is the *negotiating and administrative capacity* to design, manage and control combined financing arrangements. Otherwise joint capital development schemes will not serve the public through higher levels of infrastructure and lower costs.

There are many variations of capital investment projects financed through public-private partnerships. BOT schemes as simple examples of these arrangements demonstrate the typical actors and phases: the private sector is involved in building revenue-producing infrastructure, operates the system and after the project pays its costs; the unit then is transferred to the local government.

In a municipal BOT scheme the local government plays a crucial role, as capital project financing is based on user charges that are controlled by the municipality. Any repayments, dividends or cost recoveries ultimately stem from the tariffs paid for the service. As the infrastructure project's assets are often core, nonnegotiable municipal properties, they only partially serve the project's financing. The revenue stream is the crucial component of BOT schemes for all actors involved.

In the classical model of BOT financing there are six major actors (see figure 2) [based on UNIDO 1996]. The local government in cooperation with other *investors* establishes the project company. The equity needed to found the company comes from various sources, depending on grants, self-generated resources and other funds involved in the project. The host government provides various forms of support as an administrative, regulatory and legislative unit; such time and effort also is regarded as equity invested in the project.

The *project company* is formally the key actor in BOT schemes. It has an agreement with the owner to raise capital and the right to acquire financing from user charges. Any lending agreements are made against the project company, which has various assets: real estate, equipment, revenue-raising capacity, local government guarantees, etc. The most valuable asset is the future revenue stream from the service produced.

The future infrastructure should be built and the service managed so that the *contractor* and the *operator* are crucial actors. *Banks* together with insurers provide necessary external capital for the investment. The *users* of the infrastructure and public service are also key players. As many actors with different motives are involved in BOT schemes, there is great need for regular communication and specific agreements among them. This complexity requires consultants and lawyers during all phases of the project.

This simple scheme rarely works this way in practice, but it shows the basic relationships among primary actors. There are many combinations of roles, and often there are various organizations behind one actor (e.g., owner, contractor and financial institutions). Frequently operating companies invest in the project company, owners might be various government or funding units, local governments are involved in financing through bond issuance, and sometimes construction companies or utility companies provide loans.

In Hungary BOT schemes were developed in municipal wastewater and solid waste projects. Sewage treatment plants and municipal solid waste landfills are costly capital investments. They often are combined with improvement of the operation companies, which also require new capital and technology. In these sectors close cooperation between the municipality and the service company is behind any partnership. Typically the service organization initiates the process, as the availability of large grants make the investment fairly cheap.

In some cases, especially in small towns, one relatively large user also is involved in financing. It is in the user's interest to avoid environmental fines on water pollution, so it may accelerate capital investment implementation by lending to the municipality. The local guarantee on the service or project company loan also makes the investment process more stable and rapid. Liquidity and value-added tax (VAT) reclaim always factor as motives to establish public-private partnerships.

Figure 2
Actors and Financial Flows of Local Infrastructure BOT Schemes

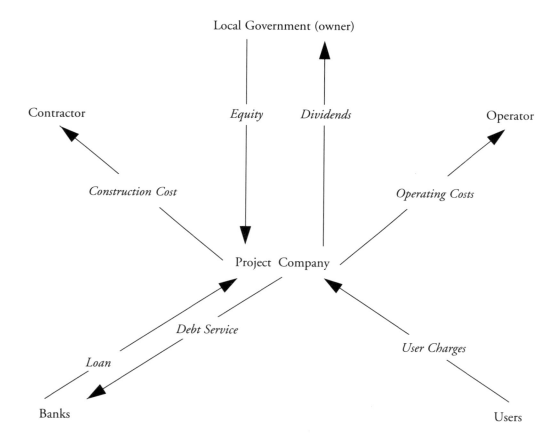

3.3.2 Ability to Pay

As user charges are crucial sources of municipal capital investment, not only the benefit principle should be applied in infrastructure development financing. It is equally important to assess the user's ability to pay service charges. By the late 1990s housing-related expenditures have increased by twenty-five percent of disposable family income. Overdue debt in the service area hit hardest—district heating—is more than twelve percent of total tariffs, and one-fifth of all customers have arrears. In other utility service areas overdue debt is lower, because the exclusion of nonpayers from the service is technically more feasible. Arrears in user charges usually are cumulated, so similar social groups are affected by several services.

Local governments have a complex responsibility in managing overdue debt problems. Beyond welfare policy measures, more efficient management techniques of service companies will help control cost increase. Local government influence on service companies can increase through fostering a competitive environment. Contractual relationships between the client municipality and the service contractor should be based on performance indicators. Output measures with local monitoring of service provision improve service quality. Increases in service costs can be controlled by more formalized contacts between the municipality and the service provider.

4   Linkages between Property and the Local Budget

In search of connections between private sector activities and the financing of local public services, fiscal and planning mechanisms will be discussed. In both areas only those techniques will be analyzed that are related to property. In this manner, new elements of local government "assets" can be developed: (1) fiscal measures (taxation, revenue policy) and (2) local planning regulations teamed with special legal institutions.

4.1   LOCAL PROPERTY TAXATION

Local taxation establishes the link between private sources and municipal infrastructure operation and development. Among the various types of taxation, property-based taxes have some particular advantages. Primarily they increase accountability; any changes in property tax rates can be related directly to modifications in the level of public services. As there is little possibility for tax evasion the beneficiary of local services is easily identifiable and visible. The benefits received can be matched with the required payments from the user of the service.

This argument is used frequently when local property taxation is evaluated from an economic point of view.

The property tax works as a "price" for the service, which supports the efficient allocation of resources in a market environment. This benefit principle works only under certain conditions. Businesses and people are mobile, so their tax capacity reflects service preferences. Positive effects of local property taxation are more visible in a municipal fiscal environment that is based primarily on local taxes and less on grants and intergovernmental transfers.

The other aspect of evaluating a local tax system is equity. Taxpayers should contribute to public expenditures in proportion to their income and wealth. The ability-to-pay principle is not easily manageable in the case of property tax. Implementation of horizontal (same treatment of taxpayers in a similar position) and vertical (different positions assume different tax burdens) equity requires sophisticated assessment methods and tax administration. Local tax on residential property might be regressive if exemptions and assessment techniques are not designed properly.

So local property tax is not the only solution for financing municipal services. But from the public sector point of view it may help to create positive feedback between municipal budgets and local property value (see figure 3).

Figure 3
Property Tax Increase and Improved Businesses

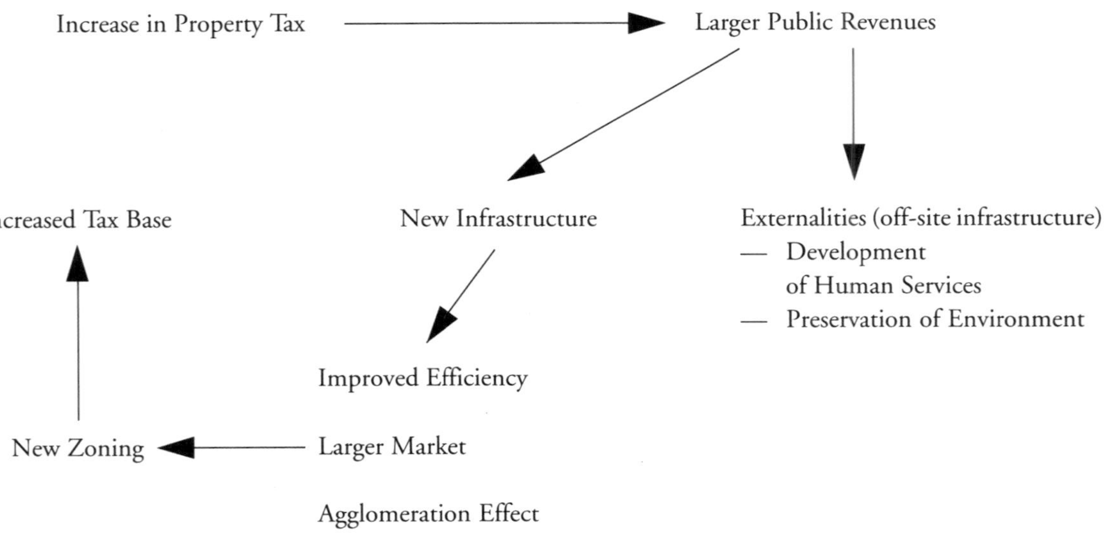

Increase in Property Tax ⟶ Larger Public Revenues

Increased Tax Base   New Infrastructure   Externalities (off-site infrastructure)
                                                        — Development
                                                          of Human Services
                                                        — Preservation of Environment

                            Improved Efficiency

New Zoning ⟵ Larger Market

Agglomeration Effect

The cycle is initiated by an increase in taxes. These revenues at least partially serve as the basis for financing local public services. Public activities of local businesses can be grouped into two categories: new infrastructure that is connected directly to their enterprises and external public services (such as human services and preservation of the environment). These off-site improvements influence local businesses indirectly.

Local government development activities have a positive impact on enterprises. Their businesses operate more efficiently, and the improved infrastructure attracts more entrepreneurs, which supports agglomeration economies and larger markets. All these efficiency gains in the private sector increase the tax base, which results in higher local government revenues.

This logic of taxation is based on several conditions. According to the economic literature on property taxation, distortions of economic activities are introduced and an excessive burden is placed on businesses. This discourages new investments and uses of capital. However, if local governments can follow changes in property value with modified zoning, then property taxes will meet the benefit principle: property owners with similar needs will be faced with a similar financial burden. The property tax works

as a tax on capital and thus acts as a benefit tax or user charge for local public services [Oates 1999; Ladd 1998]. As a side effect, property tax also will be less regressive.

Similar logic is demonstrated when local entrepreneurs launch new initiatives (see figure 4). As new capital investments put an additional burden on local governments, the local entrepreneurs should pay these costs. There are various fiscal instruments that can channel these revenues to local budgets (e.g., impact fees, special assessment and development agreements). But as the new infrastructure and better public services are available to other property owners as well, they too have to pay for these benefits. Again new zoning or special assessments will distribute the additional burden more equally on local taxpayers.

These simple schemes are discussed frequently among professionals with different backgrounds. The supporters of property taxation are divided; followers of Henry George support land taxation, which does not influence economic behavior (according to this logic, land and improvements do not have the same character). The argument against single land taxation is that it can modify the timing of development, because there are costs raised to hold the land.

Figure 4
New Development and Local Revenues

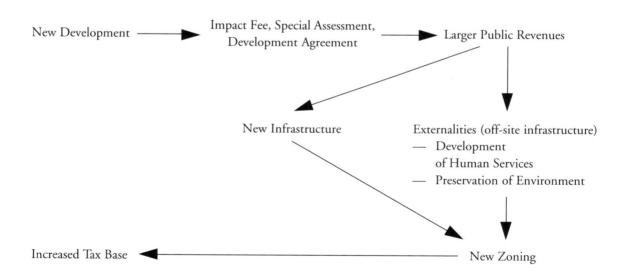

Figure 5
Spiral Development of Property Value

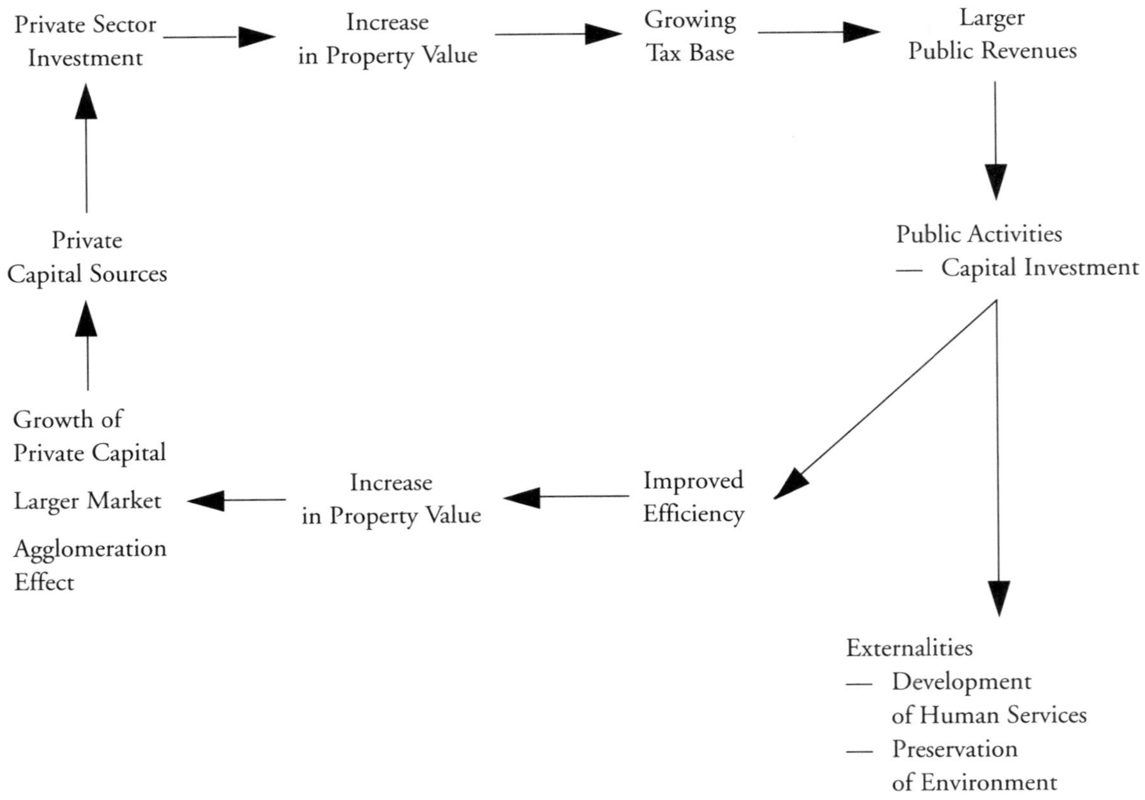

Private Sector Investment → Increase in Property Value → Growing Tax Base → Larger Public Revenues

↓

Larger Public Revenues → Public Activities — Capital Investment

Private Capital Sources ↑

Private Sector Investment ↑

Growth of Private Capital

Larger Market

Agglomeration Effect

Increase in Property Value ← Improved Efficiency ← Public Activities — Capital Investment

Externalities
— Development of Human Services
— Preservation of Environment

There are also several critics against this model from the business point of view. Their argument is that local government does not have the administrative capacity to manage these processes. Public activities that would create favorable external conditions for businesses are inefficient, so increased taxes are simply lost by local governments. Conflicts are manifest in methods of property taxation: ad valorem taxes reflect differences in tax bases much better than simple area-based taxes, but property taxes frequently are levied based on area, because tax administration is easier.

Another issue concerning ad valorem property tax is whether the tax base should be estimated by capitalization (based on the rate of return) or by using the annual rental value. The first method creates incentives for more efficient use of property because it is based on the best potential use of capital. The latter method uses the average return on capital, so there is less incentive for alternative use of the property [Davey and Péteri 1998].

In evaluating the linkages between property tax and local budgets the crucial issue is the significance of tax revenues.

Basic mechanisms might establish positive feedback between property and local public services, but when this connection is weak, other factors act against them. Property-related local government taxes are drastically different in OECD countries [Péteri and Szabó 1998]. In the federal —especially the Anglo-Saxon—countries, local property taxes are 1.8 percent of GDP. They are highest in Canada (3.9 percent) and the United States (2.9 percent). In the U.S. the average local government collects thirty percent of its revenues from property taxes. For some local governments, tax revenues are based almost exclusively on property taxes (e.g., school districts—ninety-seven percent, counties—seventy-four percent) [Ladd 1998]. In unitary countries property taxes are less significant; on average they comprise only 0.9 percent of GDP. Perhaps the local government sector is not as important in these countries as in the other group, where the states of federations are considered to be local governments.

In Hungary local taxes comprise ten percent of municipal budgets, and their ratio to local revenues significantly increased over the past decade. Property-related taxes comprise only a minor share of local taxes. Tax on buildings is ten percent; on plots (unimproved land), 1.5 percent. The communal tax on private persons is related to housing property by the number of residents, so it could be added to these figures (1.8 percent). This is the most frequently used property tax; almost one of every two municipalities has introduced it (1,525) [ÖNKORKÉP 1999].

Thus, in Hungary there is potential for revenue raising through local property taxation. In order to utilize this option and to establish a better relationship between the local budget and property, the national government has made continuous attempts to modify the national tax law. The primary goal is to decrease the importance of business tax, which operates as a local VAT and easily can be exported. The proportion of property-based local tax was to increase through the use of value-based taxation. Currently, local governments have discretion over the introduction of local taxes, and determination of the tax base is optional; thus, they almost exclusively use property area as the tax base.

New legislation is planned to support local tax administration by introducing average (and later, ranges of) values for different property groups in each county. The draft law also identifies correction coefficients with maximum values that autonomously can be applied by local governments. Tax administration is simplified, since there is no individual assessment of property; rather groups of units are the basis of the tax. This progressive amendment of tax law has not been introduced yet because local governments are still unprepared for the increased costs of value-based tax administration.

4.2   FINANCIAL TECHNIQUES

Despite the relatively underdeveloped system of local property taxation in Hungary, there are several other mechanisms for establishing financial linkages between local assets and budgets. Using the wide interpretation of assets, the authority of local governments to levy user charges and other fees is regarded as an efficient tool for combing revenues and benefits. There are two types of financial techniques: (1) public services connected to private expenditures and (2) mechanisms to link private benefits with public revenues.

In the first group local government services are financed partly by private sources through connection and user charges. In these cases the local government is the active

party and collects revenues from users of the infrastructure. In the second case private sector improvement or development projects benefit from available public services, so higher public revenues balance these private gains. Property-related public revenues are special assessments, impact fees and development charges.

These local revenues often are earmarked for special municipal activities—that is, they may be used only for the services from which they are derived. In general user charges have several advantages. They raise the awareness of the costs of the service both at the producer and at the customer levels. In this manner, they operate as a market-based regulatory mechanism, are not part of the budget and are collected by extrabudgetary units, thus making them more easily accepted by the public than general taxes. User charges also provide information on citizen preferences, and they generally are proportionate to consumption, which supports equity in financing public services [Bland 1989].

4.2.1 Financial Contribution to Infrastructural Development

The contributions of property owners to the costs of public infrastructure have been a common form of *"voluntary" dedication* in Hungary. In search of public funds to cover public utility capital investment expenditures, individual property owners in residential areas of single-family homes usually form *"community utility associations."* Such organizations provide the framework to which future users pay an agreed portion—and in many cases the majority—of the costs of public utilities to a local company that, after completion of the work, owns and maintains the specific utility system.

User charges typically cover only the cost of operational expenditures and not of future capital investment. Local governments and the service producers assume that utility investments will be financed primarily through grant schemes. During the charge-setting procedure, only depreciation costs—funding for the renewal of assets after the useful life of the equipment and real estate—are considered.

4.2.2 Special Assessment

These levies are fiscal techniques used to collect future tax revenues for public infrastructure development. Their logic is quite straightforward: infrastructural improvements financed by public sources will increase the property value of residential or commercial owners. Thus, these property owners should contribute to the cost of capital investment projects, as they will benefit from improved services.

Technically this requires clear identification of the property owners that will be affected, which is simple in the case of public utilities, but more complicated if streets are built or public lighting is installed. Another condition is the legal base for levying special assessments; approval might require a council decision or a special procedure involving the approval of the majority of affected property owners. If many small residential properties are affected, numerous administrative complications may arise. Finally, a property tax-based local government revenue system should exist to which special assessment can be linked.

Special assessments or any of the financial techniques discussed below may be connected to municipal bond issues as well. The aim is to provide up-front financing options for capital investments when the future revenue flow can be planned with high probability. Any future increase in property value, which creates higher tax revenues, could back bond issuance. In Hungary bond financing of capital investments is not used.

4.2.3 Impact Fee

Similar logic supports impact fees, which are mechanisms for financing off-site improvements—specific infrastructure capital investments or other public services (e.g., in human services). Revenues collected from impact fees should be earmarked and allocated to separate funds so that benefits and contributions can be connected clearly.

Impact fees as earmarked revenues for new developments are accepted politically by local governments. Primarily new residents or businesses are affected, which benefit from the current and extended infrastructure, so costs for the majority of residents will be lower. Impact fees do not raise property prices, and the problem of double payment does not affect investment decisions. When impact fees are established, localities usually charge less than the full cost of construction, and any increase is shifted back to land prices [Bland 1989].

Alternatively, when local economic development is a high municipal priority municipalities compete for investors. Higher costs caused by impact fees might influence investment decisions, resulting in the loss of new development options. It is necessary for local governments to compare revenues and other advantages created by business development with losses from foregone impact fees.

The act on urban planning authorizes municipalities to "*charge the expenses of roads and public utilities,* in part or in full, *to the owners of the properties concerned.*" A precondition for the utilization of this legal institution is the establishment of more detailed rules by *municipal statutes.* Parks and land for public institutions (e.g., schools) are not mentioned in the act as subject to compulsory land dedication. The 1997 act stresses that "implementation of public roads and public utilities required for the development of an area, as set by the Regulatory Plan and Local Ordinance, shall be the *responsibility of the municipal government.*" The relevant public works "shall be accomplished, at the latest, by the time the structures they are intended to serve are ready for use."

To date no Hungarian municipalities have adopted such rules. Neither the economic nor the legal implications of special assessment or impact fee mechanisms have been studied and understood sufficiently. The design of impact fees requires precise calculation of total costs of capital investment, and the final decision should result in fees less than the total infrastructural costs to avoid double payment. The collection of impact fees can be connected to permit issuance, in which case such revenues should be allocated to a fund that is used only for the capital project.

Planners have shown greater interest in tools like "betterment tax" or levies. Among Ministry of Finance officials, there has been a long-standing effort to introduce a value-based property tax on land. Both parties have tended to overvalue the potential positive effects of the mechanisms they support.

In 1997 Budapest attempted to adopt a statute on compensation when local communities and environmental groups appealed against the widening of a major road. Researchers consulting the mayor suggested the introduction of a development fee imposed on larger commercial developments along the road during application for building permits. The fee also would have served as a source for compensation to those residents whose properties were affected adversely by the nuisances of the wider road—i.e., cross-financing "worsement" with "betterment." The proposal was not even placed on the agenda of the assembly: the city is now purchasing apartments that have a view of the street.

4.2.4 Development Agreements, Transfer of Development Rights

The previously outlined financial techniques are based on already existing types of revenues, so they fit into the regular operation of municipal finances. Development agreements and the transfer of development rights are one-time actions based on bargains among the local government, property owners and new investors or developers.

Development agreements are complex deals between investors and local governments to balance the cost of infrastructure with potential public revenues. Depending on the local government's bargaining position businesses or developers might contribute to existing and extended infrastructure. In other cases, local governments are hit by economic problems so hard or need new development so badly that they pay all these additional costs. In reality local governments and developers/investors usually assume a more balanced situation, in which both parties gain advantages. Companies contribute to infrastructure and human service development, and in return local governments provide tax abatements, simpler and faster administrative procedures, support for developers in negotiations with utility authorities or national agencies, etc. (Tatabánya).

The transfer of development rights is based on the separation of development potential from the actual piece of land. Under the local government zoning regulations, one area (the "sending zone") is granted limited development in order to protect that land. The other party ("receiving zone"—the area in which higher density and concentration is desired) should buy the development rights. This way the zone under restriction is compensated for nondevelopment. The entire community benefits from these arrangements if successfully implemented.

The first condition for properly designed arrangements is to have sending and receiving areas under a long-term land use plan that capitalizes on the transfer of development rights. To promote the program a "clearinghouse" is needed that can facilitate the exchange by defining the value of the development rights and managing the transaction. Legal and administrative regulations, which tend to be complicated, present one obstacle to this process [Lane 1998].

4.3 LEGAL AND PLANNING INSTITUTIONS

4.3.1 Rules of Compensation

Hungarian lawmakers incorporated almost all rules set by the German Baugesetzbuch, including material losses resulting from the limitation of development rights by urban planning measures. Compensation is provided in the following cases:

- *change in the previous permitted use* of a property disadvantageous or unsatisfactory to the owner—compensation amounts to the extent of the decrease in property value; if the plan or ordinance was amended within three years, the owner is entitled to just compensation;
- *the property is designated for a public use*—the owner may require the purchase of the property by the beneficiary of the public interest or by the local government;
- *the property falls under a building or land subdivision ban* of a term exceeding three years—annual compensation is paid proportionate to the material loss but cannot exceed five percent of the current value of the property.

Compensation can be granted in money or land.

4.3.2 Preemption Rights of the Municipalities

Preemption rights of cities were abolished after World War II. The 1997 act reestablished such rights as having priority over any other preemption rights excluding properties with preserved buildings. A municipality is entitled to exercise *a general preemption right* with respect to the purchase of those properties that are "required to achieve the goals and targets" set by the regulatory plan and ordinance. *The right of specific preemption* refers to *undeveloped lots and areas* intended for urban planning measures that are required to achieve the "order" of urban development. The preemption rights of municipalities are recorded in the land registry.

The provisions of the 1997 act substantially deviate from those in the German law. In Germany preemption rights of municipalities are almost unrestricted in formally designated redevelopment areas and in urban development zones—i.e., in those areas where the municipality (through special development companies) is itself active in managing large-scale development projects and where betterment potentially can be the highest. This is similar to the system in France, where a declared goal of preemption rights in officially designated areas is to curtail land speculation and to facilitate the acquisition of at least partial betterment for the community in the process of implementing large-scale development projects involving public funding. In Hungary no concepts similar to the development zone or the redevelopment area have been introduced; consequently regulations for their specific handling also is lacking.

None of the municipalities surveyed are considering the introduction of preemption right provisions. In Budapest the chief architect (planner) has considered adopting mechanisms similar to the U.S. *growth management program*. Areas zoned for commercial uses on the outskirts of the city are classified in the municipal framework regulatory plan according to three distinct categories: (1) areas for immediate use, (2) areas subject to an "adequate public facilities test" and (3) areas planned for utilization in the distant future. The municipal government wanted to secure rights of preemption for itself in these zoning areas, but the districts, having a strong interest in the development of their urban fringe, succeeded in thwarting this plan.

4.3.3 Designation of Land for Local Roads

To date, the opening of new local interior streets through long—in most cases, previously agrarian—lots has been extremely cumbersome in Hungary, even if in the best interest of the majority of affected owners—i.e., new building sites created by splitting lots into two or three parts. Ministry lawmakers first wanted to reestablish the 1937 building act rule requiring the compulsory dedication of land amounting to one-fifth of the area of the affected lot as a maximum. A parliamentary commission rejected this, and a new, legally unclear provision has been adopted.

If the opening, widening or minor correction of a street *is in the interest of the owners concerned*, the municipality is authorized by law to *take possession of the land* without expropriation (eminent domain procedure), but compensation is to be paid according to the expropriation provisions of the Civil Code. Even more problematic is a second rule: *no compensation is provided* if the opening of the new road is *"upon the request" of the owners* as part of their application for a subdivision permit and *if they give up their claim for compensation.*

4.3.4 Expropriation

As discussed earlier, though handling "taking issues" (or "planning blight") caused by zoning amendments is sufficiently regulated concerning eminent domain procedures (expropriation), the 1997 act does not include any specific rules itself but refers to the Civil Code.[11]

4.3.5 Missing Mechanisms to Control Development Projects

Although the new act and OTÉK have been important steps towards a "planning and building code" adequate for the requirements of a market economy, they fail to provide mechanisms for effective control of the implementation of urban plans—i.e., the complex review of actual development projects, similar to the U.S. subdivision review or the British planning permit. The *special legal institutions* discussed in this chapter are regarded by lawmakers as mandatory *provisions to be included in local zoning and building ordinances*; their spatial implications must be represented *on the map of the regulatory plan* and—for most legal institutions—*recorded in the land registry*.

While many state administrators believe that these provisions would be well *effectuated through a series of administrative permit processes*, it is more likely that cities will be highly innovative in establishing through their municipal statutes effective, and at least partially discretionary, procedures to control larger private developments. The 1997 act's main focus is on planning and plans rather than on controlling actual processes of development.

5 Organization and Management

Modern urban planning and capital investment financing practices require new forms of cooperation between public and private actors. This relationship has an impact on the organizational and management structures of both sectors. In local governments chief architects are the focus of conflicts between private investors and representatives of urban values (planners, the building authority). Local government property management techniques can be implemented only through organizational forms that are able to combine public and private sector incentives. Obviously this requires new management schemes to ensure public control over market-based actions.

5.1 PUBLIC ACTORS IN DEVELOPMENT CONTROL

Here a short overview is provided on the main public actors involved in physical urban planning in Hungary. Only those actors that are directly responsible for local government planning and building administration will be mentioned here.

Board of representatives (legislative board)—the governing body of municipal governments, the final authority in local urban planning issues with wide discretionary powers. It is comprised of elected persons and the mayor. In cities with the legal status of counties (county seats and cities with populations above fifty thousand) and in Budapest the board is called the "general assembly." It must meet at least six times a year. The board is represented legally by the *mayor,* who is elected separately from the board.

Planning commission—a body comprised of at least one-half of the members of the board of representatives. After reviewing planning decisions, it submits them to the board. The commission is appointed by the board of representatives and cannot include the mayor or staff members. Because the majority of planning decisions are legislative acts vested in the discretionary power of the board of representatives, the commission only has an advisory role in most planning and zoning matters. Many planning commissions employ specialists with full membership rights who address multiple issues (typically,

urban development, environmental control and historic buildings preservation). The name of this body differs from place to place.

Municipal chief architect—the "chief planner" of the municipality responsible for preparing and submitting decisions to the commission on matters of urban development planning and control. In cities with county status, in Budapest and in the districts of the capital the chief architect is employed as a civil servant and must have a university degree in architecture; in other municipalities, a college degree in architecture; and in both cases, some years of professional practice as determined by law. In a few cities the chief architect has a small planning department, but in the majority of cases, consultant planners design urban plans. The indirect authority of the chief architect depends on his or her actual position in the local government and personal capacities.

Mayor's office—the administrative office of the local government composed of departments, including the building officer's department. The notary—an attorney—who employs the staff directs the mayor's office. The notary cannot be the "city manager," the tasks of which generally are performed by one of the deputy mayors.

Building officer's department—in Hungary, "*building authority.*" Until the adoption of the new law on the built environment in December 1997, building authorities functioned even in small villages. At present, their numbers have diminished substantially, and most are concentrated in cities and larger villages. Their principal task is to review building permit applications and subdivision plans and issue or deny permits without, theoretically, any sort of discretionary power (i.e., based on findings that the proposed structures do or do not comply with requirements set by state regulations—principally the state building code—and local planning documents). This department also is responsible for building inspection and for most administrative enforcement actions.

These offices, functioning in the "capitals" of the nineteen counties, perform *county administrative authority*—the legal control of the legislative and administrative activities of local governments. As building administration in

Hungary traditionally has been operated on two administrative levels, the county authorities became the "upper level" in both planning and building issues after 1994. They review the legal soundness of planning decisions made by local governments from both substantial and procedural points of view and function as *platforms for appeals* against the administrative decisions of local building authorities. In planning issues the county authorities may intervene only if they suspect illegal activities; if the case remains unresolved it is submitted to the Constitutional Court for final decision.

Special purpose authorities—sometimes the "first level" authorities in building matters. For special structures (roads, urban infrastructure, mines, nuclear plants, water engineering works, etc.) building permits are issued by bodies other than the building authorities. In areas of historic and architectural preservation, the architectural monument authority issues building permits, even for nonlisted buildings. In other cases (as in natural conservation areas) the consent of the special purpose authority is mandatory for the issuance of the permit by the municipal building authority. In urban planning matters a great number of such authorities have to be approached for expert opinions to be considered by the municipality, but their involvement cannot infringe upon the discretionary powers of the board of representatives.

Regional chief architect—not to be confused with the municipal or county chief architect; acts on behalf of the central government as a state official employed by the building office of the Ministry of Agriculture and Country Development (until 1998, the Ministry of Environment and Regional Development). Regional chief architects act in a coordinating and advisory role by transmitting and mediating central government initiatives with municipalities in planning matters. Recently their main tasks have been the interpretation of provisions of the new planning act and of the revised building and planning code.

County chief architect—counties, classified in Hungary as local governments, also employ chief architect-planners. Because counties are not considered "higher level" governments, municipal chief architects are not subordinate to them. Their main function is coordinating development initiatives and advising smaller settlements. Large cities in most cases have weak relationships with county architects.

As shown by the above list, the Hungarian system is rather one-sided, biased towards physical planning and the engineering and architectural professions, and some basic institutions common to industrialized countries are actually missing. In almost all Hungarian cities there are no actual planning departments; semi-autonomous "zoning boards of appeals" characteristic of the U.S. system also are missing. The functions of these organizations are performed through unique combinations of actors in almost all Hungarian cities.

In the coordination of economic and physical planning, property management and building administration, the case studies revealed some effective institutional solutions: a "strong" deputy mayor responsible for the coordination of all urban development; a permanent consulting group comprised of the mayor (or deputy mayor), the head of the property management department and the chief architect; the creation of government-owned or public-private development corporations; employment of an "in-house" planner to manage zoning amendments; dependence on experienced consultants functioning as "quasi-in-house" planners; close and well-controlled cooperation between the building authority and the chief architect; etc. (more about these points is discussed later).

5.1.1 Varying Roles of Chief Architects in Urban Development

The official role of chief architects is the management of urban plans and ordinances. Their involvement in concrete processes of urban development is less clear. Based on the limited information available, the following division of roles is discernable in Hungarian cities.

1. *The chief architect is responsible only for the management of official plans and ordinances.* The building authority is a separate office in city hall; the responsibilities of property management, investment and development processes fall under another department (Eger).

2. *The chief architect's office and the building authority are merged* into one single department; a separate office controls property management and development (Miskolc, Kecskemét).

3. *The chief architect is also responsible for the management of urban development;* the building authority functions as a separate department of city hall (Nyíregyháza).

The local institutional division of labor may vary substantially, but the chief architect's primary task remains the "management" of urban physical plans—in most cases, adaptation to demand of developers for building land and to the overall development policies of the municipality. The case studies clearly demonstrated that urban physical planning and plans are now in a secondary, "pursuant," position. Whether the chief architect of the city can perform a leading role in city administration or is simply instructed by the stronger actors to amend plans and ordinances depends on his or her personal professional capacities and skills.

Official planning control, however, cannot easily be bypassed in a constitutional state; thus, in most cases, the chief architect has been appointed to a small executive body, or task force, responsible for managing urban development and comprised usually of a deputy mayor, the heads of the departments of public property management and of finance, and in some cases, the director of the municipal property management company. Since until recently most decisions concerned the sale of public landed property for development, the latter officials now seem to have a leading role in these bodies.

5.1.2 Varying Positions and Institutional Links of Building Administrators

In smaller cities and villages the leader of the building authority may take a relatively strong position in the process of urban development. This is because he or she usually is contacted first with inquiries about opportunities for building. As plan amendments have become an almost ordinary procedure in most municipalities, the chief building administrator initiates the amendment process by contacting the chief architect and other responsible persons and bodies or by sending the applicant to them for more information. In none of the smaller municipalities was there a rigorous division between the roles of the "authority" and of the "council."[12]

As many building administrators are not trained architects, they tend to rely on the expertise of the chief architect if they find an application for a building permit "architecturally problematic." An informal manner of cooperation may be sending the applicant to the chief architect for an expert opinion. A more formal solution (found in one district in Budapest) is that the chief architect is contacted by the applicant for a written statement on "planning conditions." In this statement the chief architect may, in addition to listing the binding provisions included in the physical plan and ordinance, give his or her own recom-

mendations on architectural and related matters (e.g., on the alteration of the cityscape).

In large cities and in many districts of Budapest an almost total institutional separation is prevalent. If the municipality has a "strong" notary (the head of the mayor's office, who must sign all permits and other administrative decisions, as is the case in Mosonmagyaróvár), the building administrator's main concern is strict adherence to formalities and legality. These officials tend not to use even the limited discretionary powers vested in building authorities: no applications are rejected due to poor adaptation of the proposed structure to its surroundings or to poor design (as discussed earlier, some provisions in OTÉK authorize them to do so). They also are influenced by the behavior of the county administrative offices that tend to uphold decisions based on findings other than "pure law." An even more disadvantageous outcome of institutional separation is a poor flow of information between the two offices. In one district of Budapest, the chief architect's office was not informed about building and land subdivision permits granted or rejected by the building authority (quite interestingly this district is said to be most overrun by corruption).

5.2 ORGANIZATIONAL FORMS OF PROPERTY MANAGEMENT

As the transfer of property to local governments was implemented through a legal process, initially municipal management practices also were of legal character. Local ordinances regulated the decision-making and management hierarchy of property rights. It was a highly politicized scheme in which elected bodies retained most decision-making power. Local government property was categorized by type and value. Decision-making authority to sell or utilize property was invested in the mayor, committees and local council.

These structures have succeeded in maintaining public control over property management decisions, but they have failed concerning the efficient use of property. Different organizational and management techniques are needed for each of the four main types of local government property. New processes are required to incorporate property-related decisions into local government budgets. On one hand these involve technical tasks, such as establishing a property cadastre or implementing property evaluation. On the other hand, they require management decisions: regular review of available property used for public services, management of utility companies and coordination with urban development companies to utilize real estate available for investment.

Local governments were able to create modern cadastre systems for their own property by the mid-1990s. By this period the property transfer process was completed and information systems required by the national government provided a basic structure for local property registers. However, no other property management techniques have been developed in most local governments.

Evaluation methods and the assessment of core and negotiable property units do not exist. In the period of fiscal restriction, property maintenance decisions were among the first to be postponed. This led to a loss in property value or waste of municipal real estate. Public institutions seldom are evaluated from a property management point of view. There is no regular review of management practices, standards and criteria are not developed, and alternative use of assets is seldom assessed.

5.2.1 Urban Development Companies

The other types of local government physical assets are closer to the private sector. Local public utilities operate as commercial entities (joint stock companies, limited liability companies, etc.). As "profit-making" units they are forced to utilize their assets efficiently. Infrastructure is a core asset or has limited negotiable character. But companies' operating assets are subject to management decisions motivated by raising revenue through selling or renting buildings or land.

Physical assets in the municipal portfolio establish a special group of local property units. These buildings, plots and vacant land are important sources for local capital budgets. In most cases, raising capital revenue was the primary goal of local property management through the selling of assets and thus creating one-time revenues.

There are some attempts to establish long-term investment arrangements with the private sector through urban development companies. Typically business promotion is the primary goal of real estate development. Local governments are responsible for economic development, so inward investment is important for job creation and restructuring of the local economy.

Through community or regional development companies the municipality can implement effectively its economic programs pertaining to the whole community rather than to merely municipal finances. *Municipalities may use such companies to purchase strategic real properties* that can generate revenues and perform public service tasks; furthermore, this indirectly influences the local real estate market by stabilizing purchase prices and rents, which attracts additional capital.

It is a general policy principle that companies should indicate real property rather than cash in their balance sheets; the former is less sensitive to changes in the economy or inflation and better represents long-term municipal interests.

Depending on local conditions, different regional development policies may be adopted. One option is to concede more valuable areas to private enterprises. The other is for the companies to work in less popular areas, thus increasing the value of less attractive properties and decreasing local inequalities at the community level. As an added benefit, the development of less valuable lands can generate a higher profit rate with smaller investment because the relative available profit margin is greater than when increasing the value of already high value lands.

Another strategy takes the opposite route and supports the development of real estate in valuable areas. The advantage is that the property concerned serves as excellent collateral for extensive borrowing and offers excellent potential for utilization (sale, lease). The disadvantage is that relatively more capital is needed for development and for relatively less profit, though the risk of this strategy is lower than that of the previous one.

A third common strategic principle is for companies to form joint ventures, primarily with financial institutions (banks, insurance companies), or undertake development jointly with various property and regional development enterprises. Naturally, various development conceptions also may be combined.

In large cities *urban regeneration* is a goal that typically requires cooperation between the public and private sectors. In Budapest two basic models were developed in those districts most affected by problems concerning slums. Both are based on the formation of joint companies by local government, domestic and international financial institutions. The local government controls the company's decision as majority owner but operates with a strong market orientation [Urbanisztika 1997].

The difference in models used by District IX and District VIII is the role of local government. SEM-IX, the development company in District IX, is based on the French model of mixed commercial entities. The local government transfers plots prepared for market-based utilization to a company, which operates as a real estate development unit for the benefit of the district local government. A national network of these urban development companies has been launched.

The other model utilized by District VIII is based on close cooperation between the municipality and the joint stock company. Here, regeneration of residential areas cannot be implemented without the company's active involvement, and as a result, it has more influence on municipal decisions. The urban development company is involved in the design, management and implementation of the regeneration process from the very start. Thus, the company's role is broader than purely real estate development; it is involved in property management policymaking as well.

In summary community or regional development companies offer the following benefits.

1. The company receives municipal property, is granted responsibility and decision-making authority over it and is accountable for its activities.
2. The income and incentives of the managers of the company are related directly to the efficiency of the company.
3. The company deals with its business partners from an ownership position, which facilitates the exploitation of opportunities.
4. For the implementation of various high volume action plans further development companies may be established, which will be more profitable due to more efficient financial management than would be possible if the project were to be financed from the overall municipal pool of funds. In the latter case, the available development funds are fragmented by the most pressing tasks.
5. The company is an operative organization that is not constrained by internal decision-making, implementation, disbursement, administrative and management procedures of local administration.
6. The company may assume risks to the extent of its assets, which also localizes the ever-present hazard of failure, financial and prestige losses and even bankruptcy or liquidation.
7. The company as a market actor flexibly and rapidly can expand or contract financial and human resources depending on the development opportunities avail-

able. Therefore, the company also may operate with mixed ownership. Indeed, it may be more desirable to establish such companies jointly by the municipality and banks, insurance companies, construction companies, etc.

8. An additional benefit is that the municipality receives first-hand and continuous information on the market, which can then be taken into consideration when preparing or amending budgets.
9. The company and thus the municipality may engage in speculation with available property. Knowing the market and the infrastructural development level of the real estate, the market value of a particular property or area can be increased through land development and infrastructural investment, which can be turned into cash at competitive prices through sale or lease.

Finally, *the regional development company* in theory has, or should have, *no interest in being liquidated or eroding the assets* entrusted to it. The operation of the company ensures that the municipal, i.e., community property can be increased.

Democratic public administration, the controlling-testing mechanism of elections and the personal interests of elected officials and representatives require the municipality to place private property and incomes in an position in which their relative value is increased. Municipal financial management and, within this, property management also must *contribute to the increase in value of property held by other owners*, because municipal financial management is a catalyst for the fluctuation of nonmunicipal property value. Thus, the "business plan" of municipal financial management must take this into consideration. Increases in private property value attract investors, which in turn promote value growth. If property value growth goes hand in hand with investment, it engenders jobs, commercial turnover, entrepreneurial drive and the expansion of local economic bases (diversification), thus increasing real income levels.

In order to attract investors, the community must foster a favorable reputation. Details such as appearance are important, especially concerning the vicinity of incoming roads (city gates) and public spaces in general. Obviously, the value of such areas is not necessarily determined by their marketability, but rather by the indirect effect of influencing the impressions of visitors to the community. Therefore, the beautification of public spaces is a fundamental community interest, whether the direct yield of such developments can be quantified or not.

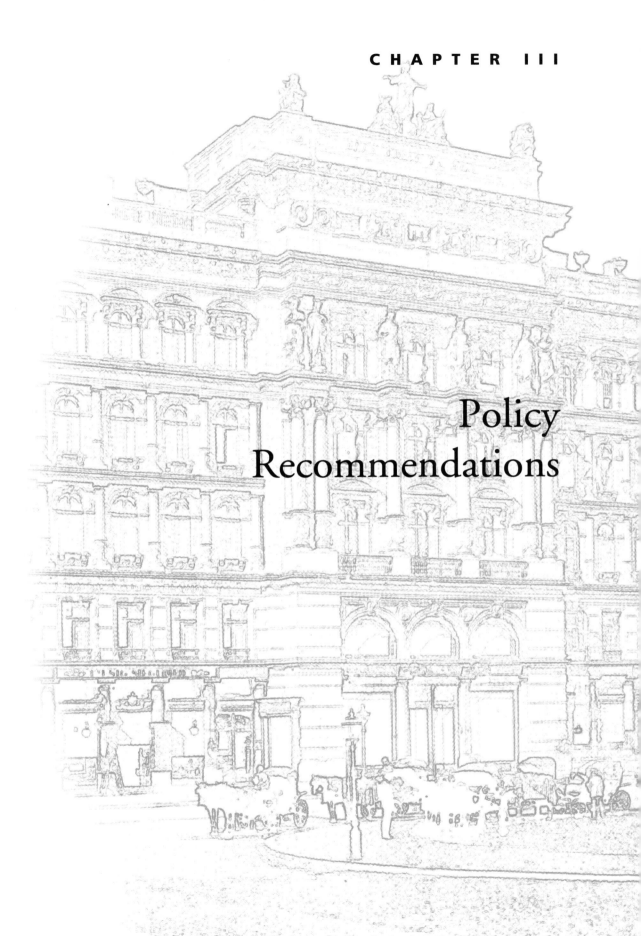

CHAPTER III

Policy Recommendations

National and local regulatory environments and management practices influence urban development planning and capital investment financing. The policy recommendations presented here are directed towards these two levels of government.

At the *national* level there are three broad types of actions necessary for the improvement of urban development. First, there are missing elements in legislation, primarily in the field of local government finances and financial management. Second, the central government should provide indirect assistance and support to local actors through a highly decentralized structure. Finally, there is a need for better information systems (e.g., cadastre, data on utility management) and training. The collection and exchange of operational models, management practices and good solutions should support this last issue.

Local governments operate in the given regulatory environment, but their management practices and technical expertise require further development. Most recommendations presented here are directed at the local level, as localities in Hungary are rather autonomous units of governments. Consequently those local officials and municipal managers who are innovative and ambitious can apply the techniques outlined here.

There are several *conditions* that influence these policy recommendations, which have an impact on the present scope of actions and influence the near future. First, urban planning practices are in the process of transformation. New legislation on urban planning and building regulation is being incorporated by local practices only now; thus, they are just being accepted and understood by local professionals and decision makers.

Second, local governments operate in a privatized market environment. The level of domestic and foreign direct investment is high, and urban services are mostly provided by commercial entities (sometimes by joint ventures with foreign partners). User charges and other benefit-related payments are used widely in financing schemes.

Third, the restrictive fiscal environment is an important factor in urban development. Local capital investments are declining, there is great pressure on local budgets to finance current expenditures, and national grants for capital investments are limited. Finally, there have been few significant changes in the organizational and management structures of localities. Under new local government legislation the formally unified municipal administration

remained rather segmented by departments or service organizations.

1 Combined Utilization of Assets

For this research and development work local government assets were used as a general term and in a broad sense. The main message for national and local policymakers is that beyond municipal *physical property*, there are three other groups of local activities that are important assets and that can provide benefits for the city: *local plans, regulations and service delivery rights* and other *fiscal and financial management techniques* (see table 9).

This study also has demonstrated that these four broad groups of local government assets should be used in a *combined way*. Urban development is based on the joint efforts of planners, regulators, property managers and fiscal and service experts. Obviously not all of the four components have to be managed together at all times, but improved linkages among them will increase the efficiency of various policy actions.

The first of the four groups of assets is *local authority and administration*. In urban development this primarily involves planning, regulation and construction permit administration. These technical activities seldom are regarded as local government assets, because they are not linked directly to local budgets or other economic benefits.

The second group, *local government property*, is regarded as a primary source of revenue for urban development. There are two types of assets: the first is directly visible real estate and related revenue sources (e.g., rents, lease); the second, general attractiveness of the city. The latter includes all external factors of urban development, such as human services, environmental protection, landscape, cityscape, etc.

Physical infrastructure is a crucial condition for urban development. Municipal activities in this area depend on national grant allocation schemes and *local management of service delivery rights*. Local governments can improve the level of public services if they utilize their exclusive authority in service provision by allocating contracts and establishing public-private partnerships.

The fourth group of local government assets includes *fiscal measures and financial management techniques*, which provide direct linkages between the local budget and property owners and service users through revenue policy. Local governments control capital investment programs and financing schemes, which are important assets if used efficiently for the purposes of urban development.

These four broad groups of assets are connected to several local *policy areas*; that is, many actors are involved in these decisions. At least six different types of professionals have an interest in urban development issues. Obviously these roles are separated only in large cities; in smaller municipalities they might be combined. Successful urban development actions do not require continuous cooperation among these professionals, but they are all affected.

In each of the four policy areas the following professions and local government units are involved in development:
1. *urban planners*, who usually are contracted by the chief architect in the mayor's office;
2. *the building authority*, which is responsible for the legal process;
3. *the property management unit*, which is often combined with *the economic development unit*;
4. *the service department*, which primarily deals with the field of urban services and infrastructure;
5. *fiscal and financial management experts*, who are involved in designing local revenue policy;
6. *capital investment managers*, who are the technical experts responsible for programming and implementing projects.

Under this framework there are numerous local actions determining *how* these four groups of assets (*what*) can be managed in the several policy areas (*by whom*). All local actions have been discussed previously. The management of local assets requires various types of actions, which sometimes need new expertise and knowledge from municipal staff and local officials.

Table 9

Assets, Policies and Actions in Urban Development—Framework of Urban Development Planning and Financing

Local Government Assets	Policy Areas	Local Actions
1. Local Public Authority Administration		
Plans, Regulations	*Urban planning*	Zoning Land subdivision Development freezes Preemption rights Redemption Appropriation Designation of land for local roads Building obligations Compensation rules
	Environmental protection	Environmental impact assessment
Administration	*Building procedures*	Issuance of building permits
2. Local Government Property		
Real Estate in Local Government Balance Sheets	*Property management*	Real estate development: review, sale, investment, lease
	Local economic development	Promoting inward investment
Attractiveness of the City	*Sectoral policies (human and utility services)*	Developing services
3. Service Delivery Rights		
Improved Infrastructure and Utilities	*Capital investment policy*	Subsidies, capital grants
	Service delivery management	Management and financing schemes: contracts, concessions, BOT
4. Fiscal Policy, Financial Management		
User Charges, Hook-up Fees	*Municipal user charge policy*	Fee-setting procedure Cost sharing, control of service companies
Local Taxes	*Municipal tax policy*	Property tax and tax administration
Special Funds, Capital Financing Schemes	*Capital improvement planning and programming*	Impact fee, betterment recoup Compensation accounts Special assessment Transfer of development rights

2   Unified Urban Development Planning

According to international theory and experience urban development planning performs three specific but inter-related tasks:

- strategy formation;
- regulatory function;
- management of urban development.

Currently in Hungary the regulatory function of planning is overemphasized, because under the evolving market economy a clear-cut provision of development rights to landowners in urban physical plans understandably has come to the fore. The strategy-forming function of planning fails in comprehensiveness and in its interrelationship with the nonphysical aspects of planning. As a reaction to former state planning and development, many munici-palities tend to behave in a passive, reactive way and to withdraw from initiating and managing even those concrete local developments that are in their vital interest by leaving these tasks to the private sector.

This unbalanced situation also is reflected in the legal background of planning: while the 1997 Act on the Protection and Formation of Built Environment covers regulatory functions in every detail, only a few provisions of law and state directives refer to the other two tasks of physical planning. Another consequence of this one-sidedness is the strongly bureaucratic nature of recent Hungarian planning and building administration. During the period of economic and social transformation of the country, there has been a strong belief that the foundation of a legally sound planning environment can be achieved better by well-regulated statutory procedures rather than by more cooperative behavior of public actors. This belief also is reflected in the strict division between the tasks and powers of elected bodies and those of the administr-ative "authorities." The former has strong, the latter very limited discretionary powers.

In order to overcome these shortcomings, the following actions are needed:

- *strengthening planning on a regional scale;*
- *boosting comprehensiveness of planning;*
- *introducing more flexible development permit procedures;*
- *establishing a regulatory framework for urban develop-ment.*

A basic precondition for the realization of these proposals is the strengthening of democratic planning institutions and of the democratic behavior of society, including public actors. As the current framework and practices respond to the prevailing conditions of transition, the above-listed goals gradually can be achieved.

2.1   STRENGTHENING THE PLANNING POWERS OF REGIONAL GOVERNMENTS

Since the political transition, the bulk of planning power is vested in local governments. Parallel to this, national state and county planning authority has diminished. In the 1996 Act on Regional Development and Planning—with a view to the availability of European Union grants and subsidies—definite emphasis was placed on regional economic development and institutions, such as regional development councils and agencies, while the authority of regional bodies—including counties—in physical planning was not clearly defined.

In the forthcoming period new regional bodies will be formed that correspond to the EU's Nomenclature of Territorial Statistical Units (NUTS). It seems inevitable that the administrative powers of these new regional bodies will be rethought, including their planning powers. In most European countries (i.e., the Netherlands, Sweden, the United Kingdom) a significant part of *strategic planning is performed at the regional level*, especially in metropolitan areas, where basic planning and environ-mental goals can be achieved better through a regionwide approach. Recent plans to introduce an overall building ban around Lake Balaton and the unclear status of the regional physical plan for the Budapest metropolitan area well reflect the seriousness of this issue.

2.2   BOOSTING THE COMPREHENSIVENESS OF URBAN PLANNING

In the forty years before the transition cities and villages in Hungary established their comprehensive (general) plans by focusing almost exclusively on centrally deter-mined development programs (decentralization of the manufacturing industry, state housing, etc.). This resulted in "plans of hope" that promptly became outdated when central programs changed. This is one of the main reasons why Hungarian municipalities have little experience in formulating plans that reflect well-conceived local development concepts and strategies.

According to the 1997 Act on the Formation and Pro-tection of Built Environment the establishment of a development concept (strategy, program) is imposed on municipalities as a mandatory preparatory element for their physical (structure and regulatory) plans. While even the most minor elements and methods for regulatory plan making and local building codes are detailed in the act and OTÉK, no rules and directives actually are established concerning development concepts. The case studies revealed that only a few municipalities have embarked on the difficult business of "vision-making." Even those that undertook the task failed to formulate a useful document.

The main difficulty in establishing a *municipal develop-ment concept* is that it must cover, although to various extents, all three main functions of urban planning listed above. The development concept on one hand should be based on an interdisciplinary and intersectoral approach and on stable values (both physical, like compactness, and nonphysical, like effectiveness and equity) that can survive election periods. Conversely the general and long-range statements of the development concept should be based upon the short-range limitations of the municipal budget and must consider those programs and projects that already have been approved.

The municipal development concept should include policy recommendations on the regulatory and institu-tional frameworks of urban development as well. These recommendations should not be restricted to the regula-tory tools of physical plans, but the document also should cover proposals for an economic-type regulatory frame-work. As policies and tools are intrinsically interrelated, a basic decision should be made in the development concept on the extent to which the municipality is going to undertake a *"proactive" role* in the development process; in other words, to what extent it is going to initiate development programs.

Experiences show that it is rather difficult to find *adequate expertise* for this type of comprehensive planning. The

employment of a wide range of consultant planners and advisors is imperative. This work must be based on thorough research, and a delicate balance should be achieved between the contributions of physical (architect) planners and of other professionals. The primary role of administrative officials is to provide data and information. When enough experience has been accumulated, it would be useful to publish governmental directives to assist municipalities.

2.3 INTRODUCTION OF MORE FLEXIBLE DEVELOPMENT PERMIT PROCEDURES

An oversimplified view of the division of roles prevails in recent Hungarian physical planning. According to this view regulations in accordance with state laws and the national building code should be established in local plans; various authorities (including building and special autho-rities), as administrative bodies with little room for inno-vation, simply have to ensure compliance with local law. Even the separation of building authorities from local governments is prevalent, and most physical planners support this.

One of the main reasons behind this strategy is the separation of expert decisions from the turmoil of local politics and, in this way, the prevention of corruption. This system is not consistent with the cooperative practices of western democracies. From the technical and proce-dural point of view it is hard to say where planning "ends" and where building administration "begins." Where is the dividing line between municipal-political and administrative-legal decision making? Despite many innovations in Hungarian municipalities, in a majority of cases "local law" has to be amended officially, even if only minor modifications of or deviations from the regulations of the physical plan are at stake.

Some of the review procedures used in almost all western democracies that make development *permit processes more flexible* and provide a *legalized platform for negotiations* with private developers will be introduced in Hungary and in other countries in transition.[13] The same holds for environmental control that, becoming a national priority in most countries, tends to depend increasingly on the exercise of authority and to limit the discretionary powers of the local elected bodies. "Unification" of plan-ning in this manner means better continuity in the permit process.

2.4 ESTABLISHING A REGULATORY FRAMEWORK FOR URBAN DEVELOPMENT

While the recommendations given thus far aim at "unification" and smoother functioning of the planning process itself, the following proposals refer to the implementation of plans—the realization of development programs and projects in the interest of the community.

As stressed in earlier parts of this study, the regulatory power of municipalities represents one of the basic assets of communities. By utilizing such authority municipalities can increase their wealth and boost economic and social development. In recent years many Hungarian municipalities have recognized this potential, but in most cases they utilize their regulatory powers only when a development project is paralleled by the sale of municipal property to a private developer or when a private developer initiates the amendment of zoning regulations.

Most municipalities, however, are hesitant to initiate any development on privately owned land because their authorization to intervene is unclear both economically and legally. This problem is aggravated by the reprivatization of agrarian land around developed areas, resulting in fragmented tenure patterns and the selling of residential property to current tenants, and also by the speculative behavior of some new private owners.

The 1997 act on the built environment includes a list of *legal institutions* (preemption rights, contributions to the cost of public infrastructure, etc.; see chapter II, section 4.3) conceived "to promote the realization of urban plans" by broadening the authorization of municipalities in specific situations. However, no rules exist concerning the procedures to be followed when a municipality actually wants to utilize its assets of this kind.

In most European countries the adoption and issuance of specific municipal statutes are preconditions to such authorizations. These statutes may be issued for greater and contiguous areas, the development of which is in the vital interest of the community and where an urgent and organized method of implementation is necessary. Special stress is placed on areas of urban renewal and large green field sites, where public intervention usually involves a substantial increase in property value and the broader authorization of municipalities is meant to curtail land speculation.

In recent years, there has been extensive debate in Hungary on the most effective economic and fiscal regulatory tools. Experts agree on the necessity of the introduction of a local value-based property tax, but there is less agreement on its usefulness as a regulatory instrument in urban development. Another question under dispute is the use of instruments that can facilitate the recapturing of at least partial betterment initiated by public development. From this point of view the key element is the degree of active involvement of the municipality. Two types of approaches and their associated methods can be distinguished from international practice for Hungarian policymakers.

- "*Proactive*" involvement: the municipality has an active role by itself or through companies (independently, in public-private partnership with a private company contracted by the municipality). This model enables more detailed planning and design. Its most frequently used instruments are *land banking, compulsory purchase, use of preemption rights and mandatory sale of land to private developers*.
- "*Reactive*" involvement: the initiator is the private sector; the public sector's participation is minimal. This model is hard to use in areas where tenure patterns are fragmented and land is not consolidated. The most frequently used instruments are *bonuses, dedications, impact fees and transferable property rights*.

Both in Europe and in the United States at least some of these tools are used as supplementary instruments to other fiscal mechanisms, such as property taxes. Their legitimacy is justified by the reasonable handling of betterment. However, most municipalities are compelled to utilize them, lacking adequate resources for public infrastructure development.

Since these are rather "rough" instruments and because they are nationally unregulated, few Hungarian municipalities have embarked on the utilization of any of them. Some legal framework provisions are needed in this field (like the Polish one on urban renewal) that also regulate in detail the legal position of those (public, semi-public, private) companies that take over tasks of municipalities.

95

3 Active Fiscal Policy

In this study, arguments for change are made in three areas: (1) improved partnership with the private sector, (2) establishment of direct links between property and local budgets and (3) more efficient capital investment programming and financing. Based on the analysis in chapter II, the most important lessons for policymakers in national and local governments are summarized here.

3.1 PUBLIC-PRIVATE PARTNERSHIP

Cooperation between local government and the private sector is the least developed in joint financing of capital investment projects. Local service delivery rights, as an important group of municipal assets, can be utilized with much greater efficiency. Under service contract schemes more private capital investments could be achieved with improved national and local government actions.

At the *national level* various forms of public-private partnerships in local infrastructure development should be supported by technical assistance. There is insufficient knowledge and *managerial capacity* at the local government level to work on complex private sector deals. Models and standard solutions are not widely known; only some cities have invented specific local arrangements. Banks and financial institutions in this rather monopolistic market are not partners in establishing joint capital investment arrangements.

Information on the critical components of partnership is not widely available for local governments and private actors. In a highly decentralized environment it is the national government's role to support cooperation through indirect measures. Local governments need comparative information on the private sector, public contracts, service charges, price-setting methods and performance indicators, which are all crucial conditions for partnerships. This information sharing should be organized by the national government through public information systems or by providing support to professional or local government associations.

In the fragmented local government structure, in which several relatively small municipalities have to establish partnerships with large service organizations, local government *cooperation* should be supported. Law defines the current legal forms of such cooperation, which do not meet the specific requirements of public-private partnerships. The main problem is a lack of joint decision-making structures. Typically the gestor or owner local government has a primary role in joint arrangements, and other participants have limited influence both in service arrangements and in capital investment schemes.

For *local governments* the advantages of private partnerships should be understood and management methods developed. Local government should be aware of the high value of their service delivery rights. These are significant assets if used efficiently in the negotiating process with the private sector. Unlike present practices, when partnerships are typically initiated by the private sector, the municipality should prepare service delivery and financial packages. This requires much professional expertise before services and capital investment projects are tendered.

One of the main obstacles of cooperation is the lack of *transparency* in local decision making. The local administration should make all stages—preparation, bidding, contracting and implementation—understandable and public. A typical argument against transparency is that it is not in the business interest of private actors. The current ombudsperson reports on toll road concession agreements made it clear that any contracts with public involvement should be publicly available. This creates additional costs for the private sector, which might be reflected in the price but definitely supports the development of joint service or capital investment arrangements.

Municipalities lack *company management capabilities.* Arms-length companies operate in a privatized environment that are not sufficiently familiar to the local administration. The main obstacles are poor contract specifications and management practices. When service departments are not able to define service standards and performance indicators, contracts serve the needs of the private sector. Monitoring performance and supervision of the service producer are crucial to the successful implementation of public-private partnership. Local governments have to respond to any failures of the contractor, or upon termination of a contract, the problems will be assumed by the client municipality.

Finally, capital investments or improved service delivery with private sector involvement will increase the service costs for users. This raises the problem of the *ability to pay*, as activities formerly funded by general revenues often are transferred to fee-based services. Thus, any changes in financing schemes require careful assessment of local incomes and user payment capacities. Joint arrangements with service producers might assist local government social and welfare policy actions. User charges should be differentiated, special compensation funds should be established, and parties should agree on techniques for managing arrears. Methods for managing overdue debt can be developed only through a cooperative planning process in which all the interested parties (municipality, private companies, users, financing institutions) are involved.

3.2 ESTABLISHING LINKAGES BETWEEN PROPERTY AND THE BUDGET

Property taxation, financial and legal or planning institutions have been introduced in order to improve the relationship between property and municipal revenues. Technical details were discussed in chapter II, section 4. Here only three general conditions will be mentioned. All require actions at both levels of government.

The introduction of *value-based property taxation* to establish relationships between local budgets and private property owners depends on the quality of tax administration. In Hungary the present act on local taxes and planned improvements in legislation provide a framework for the wide use of ad valorem property taxes. The reluctance of local governments to introduce property taxes primarily is explained by a lack of administrative capacity. The national government should participate in the assessment process by providing access to property information systems, by establishing professional networks or regional administrations of property evaluation experts and by supporting municipal tax administrators. Such indirect assistance will assist the achievement of the desired policy goals.

The financial techniques and planning institutions presented in sections 4.2 and 4.3 require two critical conditions: (1) precise calculation and allocation of costs

and (2) legal mechanisms to manage special benefits (or costs) by groups of residents or units within a municipality. The identification of affected parties also is necessary in both cases.

In the case of capital investment, costs are easily identifiable, and the *allocation of financial contributions* among users or other beneficiaries is the real task. In the case of utility services, costs are allocated by service capacity. For other infrastructure services special assessment is based on detailed analysis of the impact of capital investment. To relate this to property, revenues should reflect changes in value. When impact fees and development agreements are designed, a similar detailed cost identification and allocation process is needed. Here service benefits received by the investor should be estimated.

To separate the specific groups of residents and other property owners in the area affected by capital investment, *special forms of local government* should be established. These legal structures do not exist in Hungary, as community associations for capital investments have very limited power and negotiating capacity. The local government should support the establishment of autonomous units within the municipality as legal entities. Local administration should provide technical assistance for these independent units through their own revenue-raising and management capacities. As these "special districts" are not elected bodies, decision making requires high public involvement, clarity and a balance of interests. A fiscal and management authority should be delegated from the local government to these separate units.

3.3 CAPITAL INVESTMENT FINANCING

Details of capital investment models were discussed in chapter II, section 3.3. The two most important lessons from the analysis can be drawn here as policy recommendations. The first obstacle is the poor structure of capital investment grants; the second is the lack of local government fund-accounting practices.

The *specific grant allocation scheme* is not differentiated sufficiently to follow the diverse conditions of capital investments. The matching ratio with defined ranges of maximum value of accepted capital costs leads to cost increases and to inequalities among municipalities. To acquire the highest amount of capital grants local governments estimate the maximum level of capital costs and are not interested in cost savings. The lowest level of cost is capped with a unified matching ratio, resulting in unified capital grants for local capital investments under different technical and geographical conditions. Matching grants with various predefined grants by units of capital investment would result in the more efficient use of infrastructure funding.

Local infrastructure development projects are propelled by grant-seeking behavior. Municipalities are accustomed to their weak self-generated revenue-raising capacity, so they are unprepared for operation as economic entities that establish reserves or sinking funds for future capital investments. No fiscal local government mechanisms exist to accumulate revenues for financing future capital projects.

3.4   PROPERTY MANAGEMENT

After the transfer of property to local governments and establishment of high autonomy in the utilization of their assets, it is the local government's responsibility to develop efficient methods of property management. The national government through legislation cannot do enough in this area.

As argued in chapter II, sections 3 and 4, local governments should manage more efficiently that portion of their property allocated to service institutions or public service organizations. Methods of municipal in-house *property review* are undeveloped. A lack of good practices is explained partly by missing service strategies. As local governments do not have a strategic view on services provided, there is no clear hierarchy of goals and programs. Because of this service performance indicators cannot be specified, so there are no proper measures for the required inputs of service activities provided. Consequently real estate property available to local governments and service organizations does not match their actual needs. This could lead to the extensive use of municipal property, which might increase current budget expenditures and create the potential for unused revenue.

Regular property review is based on the identification of service needs and standards. This professional work by service experts should be matched with property available for the services. Intensively used buildings and public spaces should be evaluated on the basis of the activities performed. Ratios of property use and indicators of operation and management costs provide measures for utilization of available property. For the most expensive

and least efficient utilization of assets, service experts and property managers should design alternative options.

Internal property review would improve the possibility for local real estate development. The review process could help identify excess capacity in buildings and other real estate units. Analysis of service property should be separated from other municipal assets. This way public functions and joint activities with the private sector will not be mixed in local government decisions.

In a broad sense local asset management schemes can be demonstrated by the flow chart in figure 6, which is based on feedback between property value and public activities. The mechanisms discussed in chapter II, sections 3 and 4 establish linkages among them through municipal revenue policy, various local activities and private-public partnerships.

Some *weak points* exist in the stages of local asset utilization. The first problematic area is that local public activities are not business oriented. If local companies cannot realize efficiency gains on municipal investments, urban planning and regulations or property management actions, an important element of the chain is lost. Local governments should be more business oriented without direct ownership in commercial activities.

Another missing element in this feedback mechanism is the collection of more revenues from increased private sector activities and higher property value. Business tax is widely used by local governments, but it does not always reflect the level of local business activities. Allocation of net revenues by companies, which are the basis of the tax, does not necessarily match the actual use of local public services. Property taxes and other financial techniques mentioned in chapter II, section 4.2 would support better linkages.

Finally, both the public and the private sectors can benefit from establishing direct partnerships. Joint activities would make the outlined feedback mechanism more clear for the two parties. Public-private partnerships can be useful in three areas: in local economic development, in urban (primarily real estate) development and in the provision of public services. In the first two instances physical property is the basis of partnership. In the last, local government service delivery rights are used as assets.

Figure 6
Utilization of Local Government Assets

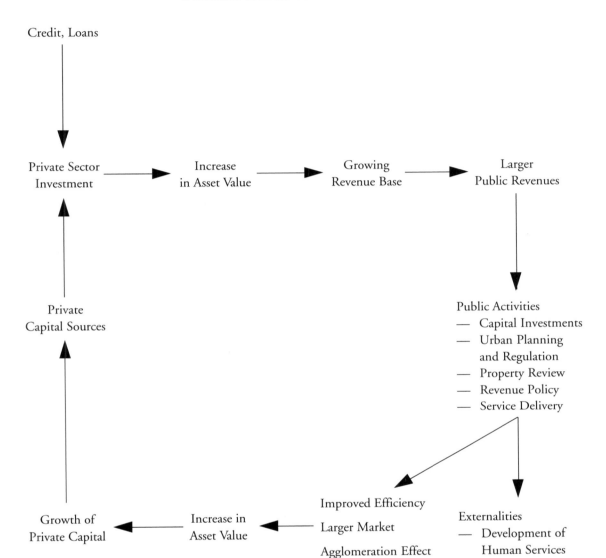

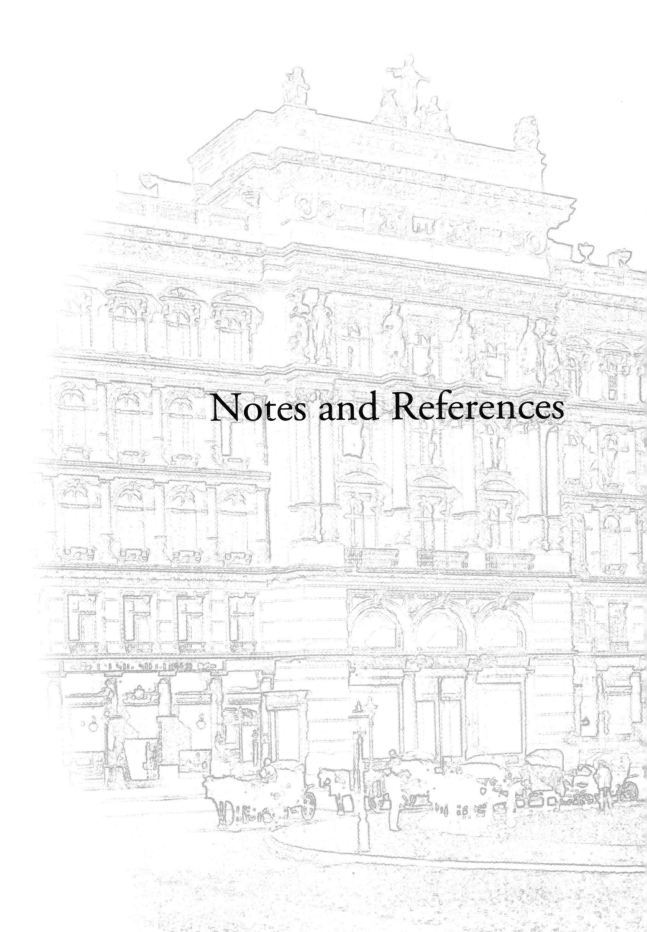

Notes and References

Notes

[1] This practice was legalized by a 1937 act and is utilized even now in a legally intricate way.

[2] Even today a Henry George Association exists in Hungary.

[3] But to be honest, if an owner of private property subjected to a radical redevelopment project could hire a good solicitor, he/she could acquire compensation—in some cases greater than the market price—for the property taken.

[4] A chief public planner of a region issued a semi-official directive that warned planners not to use any binding elements in their plans based on the assumption that all planning regulations constitute some measure of "ban."

[5] In most cases "undue process" was challenged—i.e., when the Constitutional Court stated that a building ban decision be disclosed through an administrative procedure, not by legislative decree, in order to ensure that an appeal lie.

[6] Due to its dubious relationship to the map, the ordinance will be discussed in more detail separately.

[7] Here only three special legal instruments will be presented; the rest will be discussed with urban development financing techniques.

[8] For illegal demolition or conversion of a structure listed by a local statute of conservation, seventy percent of the value is paid as a fine. In an appendix to the *1998 Government Statute on Fines* standard values are attached to specific structures that are to be taken into account when deciding the amount of fines—e.g., HUF 96 thousand per square meter of a residential building in Budapest.

[9] County local governments—seven, cities with county rights—ten, cities—sixteen, subregional units—three, industrial parks—three, total—thirty-nine.

[10] Analysis of the Budapest utilities and social housing stock demonstrated that the city actually received assets with negative value. The net worth of these assets is low in the case of substandard houses, as they have no market value due to the lack of accumulated maintenance expenditures. Under the initial conditions (management efficiency, pricing) the transportation and utility companies also had low net value [see Alm and Buckley 1994]. Later the successful privatization of the utility, water and sewage companies showed that these assets together with service delivery rights and price-setting authority turned out to be more valuable.

[11] Enforcement orders established in urban plans due to their implications on the activities of building authorities will be discussed later.

[12] As one interviewed official argued: "it is a total misconception of ministerial officials to compel us into a position of only enforcing ordinances; in a small city like ours, we have to cooperate."

[13] Procedures of this kind have been introduced also in the eastern provinces of Germany, despite the country's traditional adherence to administrative practices.

References

Alm, J. and R. Buckley. 1994. "Decentralization, privatization and the solvency of local governments in reforming economies: the case of Budapest." *Environment and Planning C: Government and Policy* 12.

ÁSZ. 1994. "Jelentés az önkormányzatok vagyonhasznosítási, vállalkozási tevékenységének vizsgálatáról." 204 (Június).

ÁSZ. 1997. "Jelentés a helyi önkormányzatok lakás- és ne lakás célját szolgáló ingatlanvagyonával való gazdálkodásának ellenőrzéséről." 359 (Június).

Audit Commission. 1988. *Local authority property: A management handbook.* London.

Baross, P. et al. 1993. *Alternative mechanisms for financing urban renewal in Budapest.* Paris: ADEF.

Bernáth, K. et al. 1999. *Önkormányzatok és a tokepiac.* Budapest: HVG-ORAC.

Bland, R. L. 1989. *A Revenue Guide for Local Government.* Washington, D.C.: ICMA.

Chandavarkar, A. 1994. "Infrastructure finance." *Policy Research Working Paper* (The World Bank) 1374.

HMSO. 1989. *Urban regeneration and economic development.* London.

Horváth, M. T. et al. 1994. *Javaslat Budapest új közigazgatási rendszerére.* Budapesti Negyed.

Jókay, K. et al. 1998. *Municipal Infrastructure Financing in Hungary: Four Case Studies.* The World Bank, SNDP.

Ladd, H. F. 1998. *Local Government Tax and Land Use Policies in the United States. Studies in Fiscal Federalism and State-local Finance.* Cheltenham, U.K., Northampton, Mass.: Edward Elgar.

Lane, R. 1998. "Transfer of Development Rights for Balanced Development." *Land Lines* (March).

Leithe, J. 1990. *Impact Fee Programs.* Washington, D.C.: GDOA.

Locsmándi, G. 1997. *Property rights and urban planning in Hungary—a procedural analysis.* Universite Aix-Marseille.

Locsmándi, G. 1997. *Városfejlesztés és tervezés Budapesten.* Budapest: Megyei Évkönyvek, CEBA Kiadó.

Locsmándi, G. 1994. *Javaslat az építési tilalommal összefüggo kártalanítások kezelésére az új építési törvényben.* Budapest: BME.

Locsmándi, G. 1993. *Planning the Environment—A European-American Comparative Study.* Baltimore.

Locsmándi, G. et al. 1996. *Javaslat a Fővárosnak városfejlesztés gazdasági szabályozására.* Budapest: ÉrtékTérkép Bt.

Lukovich, T. 1997. *Egy új világ körvonalai: a kereskedelem és a város átalakulása.* 7–8 szám.

Magyar Hírlap. 1998. "Terjed a mallmánia" (Február 20).

Miles, M.E. et al. 1992. *Real Estate Development: Principles and Process.* Washington, D.C.: Urban Land Institute.

MIS Report. 1989. "Establishing a real estate asset management system." *ICMA* Vol. 21, No. 4.

Oates, W.E. 1999. "Local Property Taxation: An Assessment." *Land Lines* (May).

ÖNKORKÉP. 1999. "Adó- és illetékbevételek 1998-ban." (Március).

Péteri, G. and M. Lados. 1999. "Local Property Taxation in Hungary." In *Property Tax: An International Comparative Review,* ed. W. McCluskey. Aldershot, U.K.: Ashgate.

Péteri, G. and L. Szabó. 1998. "Ingatlanadózás—nemzetközi összehasonlítás." Kézirat.

Péteri, G. 1997. "Alternative Service Delivery." In *Public Finance. Theory and Practice in Central European Transition,* ed. J. Nemec and G. Wright. Slovakia: NISPAcee.

Péteri, G. 1996. "Changes in Management of Local Services." In *Arena and Home,* ed. T. M. Horváth and J. Kiss. Budapest: PTI.

Péteri, G. 1996. *Local Government Capital Improvement Programming.* Budapest: LDI Foundation, Local Government Know-how Program.

Péteri, G. 1995. *Municipal Financial Management. New Possibilities, Economic Methods.* Budapest: LDI Foundation, Local Government Know-how Program.

Renard,V. and J. Comby. 1990. *Land Policy in France.* Paris: ADEF.

UNIDO. 1996. *Guidelines for Infrastructure Development through Build-Operate-Transfer Projects.* Vienna.

Urbanisztika. 1997. *A SCET–Magyarország Városfejlesztő Rt. célkitűzései.* 4 Évf., 7 Szám.

Summary of
International Comparison

This report aimed to study the relationship between urban planning, local government property management, municipal service delivery rights and capital investment financing practices. These components of urban development are relatively developed in Hungary, which has a longer tradition of market systems and decentralization. Based on these experiences LGI planned to invite more countries to participate in an international comparative project.

To assess the feasibility of the approach used in Hungary and to specify problems in some countries of the Central and East European region a survey was conducted in four countries. Four teams were asked to provide basic information on the issues discussed in the Hungarian report and to identify the most important areas for urban development in their own countries. In this annex the lessons from the country reports for Bulgaria, Romania, Slovenia and Ukraine are summarized.

1   HOW TO CREATE
A REGIONAL PROJECT

After the first round of basic information collection and consultation with our partners in the four selected countries, it became obvious that one cannot run a classical international comparative project on this issue. Local basic institutions, legislation, finances and motivation are so diverse in Central and Eastern Europe that no common methodology can be developed for the participants. Not only the formal structures and procedures seem to be rather different, but also the experts of the same profession (i.e., urban planners, local finance specialists, property managers) do not speak the same language.

So it is problematic to collect systematic information on available assets in various countries, primarily because fiscal and property-related data are not reliable. The rules of the game in local policymaking and the procedures of municipal administrative decisions are influenced by the political and economic roles of local governments, and there is great discrepancy in this respect. In the urban planning process the influence of various actors cannot be assessed without a deep understanding of the environment of the public and private sectors.

Consequently any "forced" joint framework for regional research would be too general to incorporate the different local systems of each country in the region. Future project management costs would be too high to harmonize

research efforts in several countries. The outcomes would not be satisfactory or useful for any of the participants, because comparative information would be too superficial for each of them.

The regional character of the project should be designed in a different way. As the countries participating in the first round of the project expressed their interest in future cooperation and urban development was regarded as an important issue, *we should rely on local initiatives*. Each country participating in the future "regional" project should identify the most relevant problems for the research and development program.

Based on the country project proposals, the regional program should have three functions:

* to assist and encourage the in-country research teams to work on those issues that are of *greatest interest to other countries* in the region;
* to support *coordinated information exchange* among participants on locally studied issues;
* to highlight the "common denominators" of the country-specific research and development programs in order to *formulate the characteristics of the region* or groups of countries in the region; this way the regional report will be less important, but the work within the countries would support the development of locally viable solutions.

2   TOPICS FOR FUTURE
REGIONAL RESEARCH

Based on the country reports it is quite evident that different aspects of urban development should be researched and improved jointly. Thus, *legislation, institutions* and *practices* must be the *combined* focus. National and local policies on urban development are very much dependent on the legal environment. Shortfalls in daily operation and practices are explained by the lack of clear legislation on property, local government functions and management. There are missing institutions in these countries, which hinders the proper relationship between municipal finances and local assets. Fiscal instruments and the real estate market can be developed with systematic work in national and local governments. Management and administrative processes are also integral parts of urban development. In summary, future research and development projects should focus on all three aspects of the problem: *what* should be accomplished to improve urban development in the region, *by whom* and *how*.

Table A2
Country-specific Urban Development Topics and Issues

Strengths, Positive Elements	Weaknesses, Missing Components
Bulgaria	
Privatization at the local level Value-based real estate tax Developed urban planning and administration systems Council for TUMA location/technical permit Environmental impact assessment	Limited local autonomy (lack of legislation and budget) Municipal property under concession only Earmarked privatization revenues Capped self-generated revenues for capital investment Local firms as public institutions Low scale public-private partnership
Romania	
Property-related taxes Building permit law Planning certificate/building permit	Local autonomy in implementation Legislation on property rights Limited planning and permitting authority Delayed concession law No public-private partnership
Slovenia	
Advanced municipal finances Capped local property tax Developed planning legislation Supportive environment for SME development	Unresponsive urban planning Planning and permitting separate Centralized capital financing Lack of local coordination of funds Service provision: public trading services law
Ukraine	
Tapping natural resource revenues Municipal property fund	No discretion on property Double subordination in planning High indirect costs Distrust of private sector Dominant administration Outdated urban plans

The project proposals are based on the three broad categories of local government assets: (1) financial, (2) regulatory and (3) urban planning issues. This list is based on the country reports; thus, it cannot be regarded as complete, but rather as the first inventory of problems in urban development.

2.1 Local Government Finance

1. Real estate management

Legislation usually separates two large groups of municipal assets: public property and private (commercial) property. The purpose of this separation is to limit local government discretion in selling and managing these units. The distinc-tion between the two groups of property is the first issue for further research (where do utility networks and social housing—for example—fit). The second—perhaps more important for practice—issue is how these two types of municipal property are managed by local governments. Management methods of public municipal property (service institutions, public buildings and areas, etc.) especially are poorly developed. These public real estate units are regarded as property without value, so they hardly can be incorporated into traditional property management systems.

2. Development of real estate markets

Efficient urban development systems require intensive cooperation between the public and private sectors. One

107

condition of this partnership is a highly developed real estate market. An important topic for the future research and development project is to identify who the present actors in real estate business are and determine their motivations and practices. The role of national and local governments in nurturing this market also should be analyzed: how they can influence market development and what are their means of control. Here various techniques of local regulations (e.g., zoning), lease and auction schemes, administrative procedures, excise duties, information systems and transparency of local decisions are the crucial problems.

3. *Property-related local revenue*

Increasing self-generated revenue is a critical condition of developed local government systems. Urban development especially needs close links between local budget revenues and property-based municipal actions. Taxation and other charges and fees related to property management are typical methods of providing connections between public and private spheres of the economy. However, changes in local taxation should be coordinated by national policy; otherwise, the decentralization of taxing authority only will increase the general tax burden. As property-based taxation requires rather sophisticated tax administration, this is a critical issue for any policy research in this area.

4. *Capital investment financing*

Local government capital investments have strong influence on urban development. The municipality has an impact not only by building new service, housing and administrative units, but also indirectly by developing the physical infrastructure. The current low level of capital improvement is primarily directed towards basic utility services, roads and transportation.

Methods of financing local government capital investment are topics for future research. Local finances are dependent on national grants, especially where capital budgets are separated at the local level. Various grant schemes (matching grants, earmarked revenues, capped capital expenditures, extrabudgetary funds) and allocation methods (normative, unified, discretionary) are issues to be discussed. As local government borrowing is rather underdeveloped in these countries, research on the main conditions for improving credit markets is a large area for further work.

2.2 Regulatory Environment

5. *Relationship with public utility companies*

Urban development in a broad sense can be interpreted as management and improvement of municipal assets. Local government as a regulator of public utility companies has a crucial role in developing these assets. Several issues are relevant in the region, and the diversity of practices can instigate the productive exchange of information. The most important problems are the following: state or local ownership of these assets, legislation and daily practices of contractual (concession) relationships with service providers, local government influence on utility companies and municipal decision-making procedures, price-setting authority, charging techniques and tendering regulations.

6. *Public-private partnership*

Local governments operate in a market environment, and private economic actors influence their operations in several ways. Local governments are forced to cooperate with local investors; large infrastructure capital investments require joint financing of public projects. In most of the countries legislation, institutions and practices for active and balanced partnership with the private sector are missing.

2.3 Urban Planning and Administration

7. *Legislation on urban planning*

Regulations on urban development and municipal practices were developed during the period of state monopoly and ownership. The new market environment requires more flexible urban planning systems and control mechanisms for public actors. The hierarchy of urban plans should allow the development of local incentives, as the scale of centrally financed capital investment is reduced. Planning regulations have to support municipal adjustment to the needs of the local economy and provide instruments for establishing partnerships with local private actors (investors, developers).

8. *Urban development administration*

There are three major components of efficient administration: proper information for decision making, professional and transparent procedures and effective enforcement of local decisions. Information for urban development is provided partly by national systems (cadastre) and is partly locally managed (property registration and municipal inventories). The decision-making process on urban development projects (planning, issuing permits) requires coordinated efforts of at least three strong units of the local administration: finance, property or sectoral departments and urban planners. Public involvement in these decisions is crucial as capital projects are financed locally.

9. *Managing specific urban planning problems*

In this period of rapid change in property rights and in the emerging market environment there are three major problems that were raised by the country reports. First, rapid and uncontrolled growth of urban areas is mentioned. Land privatization and restitution of state-owned property, the decline of social housing and the increasing costs of existing blocks of flats influence this. Second, parallel to urban sprawl, the increasing illegal use of land and construction is mentioned as a problem related to private sector development. Finally, economic transformation initiated changes in land use, which are most visible in two areas: agricultural land is used for residential or commercial purposes, and the decline of industry resulted in huge areas of derelict land.

These broad topics for future research give a framework for potential regional projects on urban development. As the participating countries will define the character of the research and development program, these common issues cannot be forced on individual teams. However they could serve as a checklist for the Local Government and Public Service Reform Initiative (LGI) in evaluating and selecting country project proposals.

3 EXPECTED OUTPUTS AND PROJECT MANAGEMENT

There are three major outputs of the planned regional project on urban development:

1. *Comprehensive information* on various aspects of urban development in individual countries. Major

legislation on local government finances, municipal property and public and private institutions working with local governments assets should be collected, preferably in English or Russian. Procedures at the national and local government levels should be evaluated, as laws and administration cannot be understood without careful analysis of daily practices.

2. *Policy advice* at the national level is important in the long process of legal and institutional change. Solutions for each country should be developed internally using their own intellectual resources. However countries with a varying speeds and directions of development, but with a similar heritage of the "socialist" past, could benefit from experiences in other countries.

3. *Local practices* and methods of urban development should be compiled from the most innovative public or private entities. Evaluation of critical conditions for good practices is needed; otherwise they cannot be replicated under different circumstances. Survey methods and techniques of dissemination within the countries and among different systems should be part of the project at the national and regional levels.

Research methods for the future regional projects on urban development should support the expected outputs of the planned work. This type of research and development project fits into the new role planned for LGI. Launching a regional project without a strict comparative character, but with strong coordination is suitable for LGI. This way country projects can be kept under some control and LGI would be able to initiate local processes by supporting the most relevant topics.

LGI's role in the future program should involve a *two-stage process*. First, LGI should coordinate the initiation of projects in different countries through grant schemes and provide advice on project design and implementation. Afterwards, continuous coordination among the country teams and with experts from other regions should be provided.

In the second stage of the regional project, when results are available, information exchange is necessary. This requires professional evaluation of the analysis performed and the circulation of research that is internationally relevant to the participants. General lessons of parallel efforts also should be summarized.

109